MORE FUN AND ENTERTAINING BOOKS FROM JEN HATMAKER!

Acknowledgments

I want to thank my husband, Brandon, for cutting me a lot of slack on my roles. Thanks for not pointing out the things I wrote about that I've yet to master. I plan on having it all sewn up by the time I'm fifty or something. For being patient in the meantime, I love you.

My girlfriends deserve line space for taking the journey with me. I've never known a group of girls who try so hard, even if we mess up the worst. I don't want to think about living one day without you. You are the quirkiest Modern Girls, and I adore you.

I can't fathom what this study would look like without my editor, Karen Lee-Thorp. You can spot a rambling rant with unmatched precision. Sorry I do that, but I'm incapable of changing. Just keep your delete button in good working order.

To my talented friends at NavPress: Terry Behimer, Kathy Mosier, Mike Kennedy, Kristen Baldini, Kris Wallen, Arvid Wallen (love my covers), Pamela Mendoza, and every other dear person who touched these projects of mine. I can't tell you what a pleasure it is to work with you.

Finally, I am infinitely grateful to You, God, for loving me, though I'm a bit of a problem child. Thank You for giving me

security and grace in my roles. I've never felt too far gone, and that is a credit to Your merciful patience and affection. I love You as much as any daughter could.

Contents

For every woman who has held a baby while stirring dinner, taking a phone call, helping a kid with home-work, thinking about work the next day, and gearing up for sex that night. May this study be the equivalent of an unexpected housekeeper, chef, and secretary showing up on your doorstep. I love you, Girlfriend.

Introduction

Welcome, Modern Girls! An informal poll of girls in my life revealed balancing our roles as a top struggle for women across all ages and stages. As God confirmed that this indeed was my next topic, I went into the fetal position. When I told one girlfriend about this upcoming project, she said, "Fantastic! Who is going to teach you?" Touché.

I don't know why, but God called me into ministry now. He didn't let me get older so I could know stuff. So I'm always teaching what I'm currently learning. Know this: I've read fifteen books, taken weeks off to prepare my head for this writing, and dragged countless women into conversation because, Girls, I am so in the trenches with you. One author I read actually wrote, "I never understand why women struggle in this area so much." *What?* Is she on drugs? And if so, will she share?

She obviously does not live a real life, so know this about me: I'm a pastor's wife, a mom of three (ages eight and under), a friend, a daughter, a sister, a writer, a teacher, a neighbor. I have no nanny, no housekeeper, no parents in town, no assistant, no free babysitters, no free ride, no time, and often no clue. So I won't be writing while the nanny takes care of my kids and the maid cleans my house. I'll be typing with a

three-year-old lying in my lap putting tape on my face.

I know how insane it feels to juggle fifteen roles. If you've ever bawled your eyes out from sheer exhaustion, this study is for you. If that seems a little dramatic, you can read the author I referenced earlier. She doesn't get us either. But if *frazzled* has ever been used to describe you, let's reclaim beauty together in our roles: believer, wife, mother, professional, daughter, and friend. I'll be your girlfriend, not your lecturer. Through healthy boundaries, diligence, and freedom, we'll discover together that we "can do everything through him who gives [us] strength" (Philippians 4:13). We really can. God's not a liar.

You'll encounter three icons throughout the study representing three different ways to respond. The radio icon 📻 indicates a time to dig into the Word, the rearview mirror icon 🪞 offers a chance to personally reflect on truth, and the telephone icon ☎ opens the door to intimate prayer. The questions with asterisks throughout the study are good discussion starters if you'll be meeting with a small group. In addition to the book you're holding, you'll need a Bible and a lined journal for your answers and journaling activities.

From one busy Modern Girl to another, enjoy.

WEEK ONE

Jacked Up

Chains

To show you how qualified I am to be in this club, let me tell you about this very morning. I will try not to embellish at all.

We woke up late with only twenty minutes to get the family out of bed, dressed, fed, and out the door. Because my husband, Brandon, was driving the car pool to school, he jumped in the shower, leaving me to orchestrate the three-ring circus of the kids. Jen the Siren was feeling guilty for not showing up in bed last night, so she didn't fuss. Jen the Mom dragged children out of bed, threw clothes at them, and tried to not implode upon hearing, "That tag is too itchy"; "Those pants feel too slicky"; "Why do I have to go to school every day of my life?" There might have been more clothing options if Jen the Maid wasn't so sick of laundry.

One minute later, my oldest son erupted in horror when he discovered that Jen the Tooth Fairy had neglected her duties because she fell asleep on the couch at nine thirty. Daddy covered for her absence saying that sometimes the Tooth Fairy's GPS system malfunctions and she ends up in

Connecticut. While our neighbors waited for ten minutes, Jen the School Manager threw one bag of peanut butter chips for the hundredth day of school, two permission slips, one ten-dollar field-trip fee, three sign-up sheets for the school carnival, two school evaluation forms, a bead project for the aforementioned hundredth day of school, and hastily made lunches (crusts on) into backpacks and pushed everyone out the door.

Believing I deserved a shower, I stole ten minutes for one, grabbed some clothes off the floor, and raced my littlest to preschool with wet hair and no makeup. The mom in front of me was wearing, so help me this is true, a cheerleading skirt (*perhaps* tennis) with a perfect blonde ponytail and manicured nails. I looked like I was homeless.

Driving home, I was preoccupied with managing the end of this week, as I'll be gone for three days. Jen the Teacher needs a sub to lead her Bible study, Jen the Mom is still trying to fill two holes in the child-care schedule, and Jen the Unpaid Teacher's Assistant needs to convince another mom to fulfill her Friday morning duty at the kindergarten paint table. Meanwhile, Jen the Writer knew she'd begin writing her next Bible study this morning. Pondering all this, I found myself driving twenty miles under the speed limit. That's a miracle on par with a talking donkey.

Oh, Girls, I've told my husband it would take fifteen women to fill my roles. He tries to be impervious to my melodrama, but he knew what he was getting into when he married me. It is hard work to be me. It's probably hard work to be you, too. Between the responsibilities we shoulder and the positions we fill, it sometimes feels like we alone keep the world spinning. We're tired. We worry. We wouldn't be so overwhelmed if each role wasn't so vital. How can one measure the worth of a mom versus a wife? A professional versus a friend? A servant

of God versus a daughter? We're all those things. And they all matter.

 When it comes to balancing your roles, how do you feel right now? Why?

As usual, God's Word is not silent. Watch this: When the prophet Isaiah was born, the Holy Land was in two parts: Israel in the north, Judah in the south. Isaiah's fellow prophets worked the north. Their message was this: Repent, or you're going down, namely at the hands of Assyria. Of course, Israel had a history of selective listening, so they were captured by the Assyrians in 722 BC. The nation of Israel was eradicated, never to be restored as it once was.

God told Isaiah that Babylon would do the same to southern Judah if the people didn't shape up. They had reached His threshold for idolatry and rebellion. Still, God sent not one, not two, but seven prophets to Judah, begging them to repent. Yet ultimately Babylon captured Judah in 586 BC.

 *Do you ever feel like you're captive to or trapped by your roles? If so, which ones feel like chains? You can be honest.

Do you have any ownership in this? Has God been trying to warn you? How?

Before Babylon invaded, Judah felt safe, unconcerned with God's blathering prophets. Yet not only did God tell Isaiah the details of their capture, but He also threw in the words of comfort they would need after their seventy years of captivity were over (Isaiah 40–66). *God offered words of restoration before they were even captured.* That's how much He loved His people, and we'll be studying those healing words today.

Most of us aren't living in deceptive peace like Judah was.

We're on the other side, desperate for God's help. We are aware of our chains. Some of us have dragged them around for years: the chains of obligation, frustration, compulsion, and weariness. No one applauds the way we mop. There is no gratitude expressed for digging into the algebra archives as we stumble through "new math" with our kids. Our professional accomplishments are met at the door with, "What's for dinner?" Meanwhile, our favorite friends—including God—suffer from neglect while we spiral in guilt. We might feel better if one person noticed how hard we're trying.

Read Isaiah 40:27. How do you honestly think God regards your frustration? Do you think He's more "big picture"? Be truthful.

The JHV (Jen Hatmaker Version) says, "O Jen, how can you say the Lord does not see your troubles?" God cares greatly about our frustrations because they affect our roles, and our roles shape our relationships. He is concerned with the little pieces because together, they form the whole. When He finds us exhausted and discouraged, He cares.

And He can make it better.

Read Isaiah 40:28. Why would God say this to people who've been in captivity for seventy years?

I love when God says, "His understanding no one can fathom." Yes, He understands physics, universal properties, holiness, eternity. But do you know what else He understands? Me. He's a Parent, a Friend, a Bridegroom, and a Laborer, too. He knows what it's like to work endlessly, sometimes to no avail. If ever anyone had to be everything to everybody all the time or the sun would stop rising, it's God. Just check out any page in the Old Testament for a sampling of God's frustration.

He gets your weariness. He appreciates your fears. He understands your aggravation when you feel more like a maid than a wife. He has sympathy for your fatigue. God realizes your professional passions. He shoulders your cries when you can't seem to get to any of them. Certainly He identifies with every tear shed over your children—when they disappoint you or drive you mad.

His understanding no one can fathom.

*Read Isaiah 40:29-31. The original word for *renew* (verse 31) literally means "to exchange." What is God communicating to you through His Word?

Does this seem implausible to you? Do rest and hope and strength feel unrealistic? Believer, walk with me for the next six weeks. If the Lord *created* a woman to be a servant of God, a wife, a mother, a professional, and a friend—not forgetting that she is still a daughter—then there is a way to be that woman. He didn't create us for failure nor destine us for frustration. It's not His way. He is beckoning us from captivity. His words lead us to restoration. He gives strength to the weary and increases the power of the weak. If that's you, welcome. God can set you free.

> Comfort, comfort my people,
>   says your God.
> Speak tenderly to Jerusalem,
>   and proclaim to her
> that her hard service has been completed. (Isaiah 40:1-2)

Are you worn out, Friend? Thank God for bringing you to this study, however you got here. Ask the Spirit to prepare you for radical change in your heart and life.

The Thing About Wineskins

I'm a reluctant convert to technology. As recently as two years ago, I was writing out my talks by hand. With a pen and paper, I'd research, write the first draft, edit, and then crank out the finished product. You should see how many notebooks I filled. From my first notes to last draft, one talk would take up thirty notebook pages. Wasn't I clever?

My husband stood shaking his head over my notebooks one day and said, "Why are you still preparing like this? Do you have any idea how much time you're wasting? Join your generation. Let me introduce you to Mr. Laptop." I later discovered that publishers don't care for handwritten manuscripts either, so the notebooks were retired.

Times change. For the most part, I'd say change is good. Give me one day in the twenty-first century over every day as Laura Ingalls Wilder. I like where we are. I love what we can do. I'm a fan of voting and Starbucks.

Here's the key: We must mentally adapt to the times we're living in. Though women say otherwise, we cling to antiquated images of the ideal woman. Yet the culture we're living in has radically changed, and the notebooks from yesterday can't keep up.

Part of our problem is our moms. And our grandmas. How did they do it? Why don't their models work for us? Sheila Wray Gregoire wrote, "Things are more difficult than they were when our mothers were young! It's not that your mother and grandmother did a better job than you do, but that they did a *different* job."[1]

*How is your world different from your mother's world? Think in terms of needs and expectations regarding:

Your marriage

Your children

Your career path

How do those differences make your roles harder today?

Almost universally, our barometer rises and falls in comparison:

"My grandma made pie crusts from scratch."
"My mom sent four kids to college."
"Our house was always clean."
"My mom's head could swivel 360 degrees, and she never slept."

Read Matthew 9:14. Deep down, why do you think John's disciples asked this of Jesus?

Essentially John's disciples asked, "Why do we have to work so hard, and your disciples don't? Isn't fasting what we're supposed to do? This isn't fair." The duties of religion had become a source of frustration.

As for the duties of womanhood, it might sound more familiar like this:

"Why am I taking care of everything?"
"Why didn't my mom seem this busy?"
"My dutiful performances aren't getting noticed."
"Why do others seem free, while I feel burdened?"
"This isn't fair."

I've said it all. I've wondered why God would make me do all this stuff and then not care when it turns out to be impossible. I've even gotten in His face and demanded justice. And worse, I've been sure He was mad at me for my poor performance. I could see Him shaking His head, sadly declaring, "Beth Moore writes studies *and* keeps bathrooms clean. She's My favorite."

After barely dignifying the question with an answer, Jesus spoke a short parable that, frankly, I didn't get for years. But, Girls, you're gonna love this. Read Matthew 9:16-17.

Here's the deal: In ancient times, goatskins were used to hold wine. Brand-new skins had the ability to stretch. Think of them as a precursor to spandex, the Devil's fabric. At some point they reached their stretching capacity and remained that size forever. So old skins were already stretched out.

Brand-new, unaged wine also expands. Once it is poured into the container, the fermenting process builds up pressure that causes this expansion. It's why a cork pops out of a wine bottle like it does (*so I've heard*). This new wine was poured into new wineskins because they expanded together.

Stay with me. If an old, stretched skin had a tear, it had to be patched with old, stretched skin. If you used new skin, the second the patch would stretch, it would pull the stitching out and make the tear worse. Similarly, if you poured new wine into old skins, when it fermented and expanded, it

would burst open the old skins that couldn't stretch anymore.

Summation: Old had to stay with old; new had to stay with new.

What do you think Jesus was explaining to His original hearers in Matthew 9:16-17?

For you in the generations before me, forgive the following analogy. Jesus said it first. Girls, the women who've gone before us are stretched skins. And do you know what they contain? Aged wine: a blend of expectations and experiences that characterized their generation. It was once all new, but their roles expanded with their lives and times.

At some point, their growth process reached maximum capacity. Any pesky new wine didn't fit. Try explaining your discipline techniques to your grandma. Certainly it was good aged wine, but it has run its course.

*In fulfilling your roles, what happens when you try to contain the new wine (circumstances and experiences) of your generation in old wineskins (methods and expectations of previous generations)? For instance, do you work outside the home but try to parent like your stay-at-home mom did? Do you feel guilty because you manage less for your husband than your mom did for your dad? In your life, what does this tension look like?

Believer, we are the new wineskins. We're younger, still stretchable. But the scenery has changed, and our landscape is different. We are being filled with the new wine of *our* generation, and it's expanding. We know that pressure well. One baby turns into three. Financial stress escalates. Career demands swell. Life gets bigger. We're created to stretch with these changes, but many of us are bursting because we've accepted old wineskins as our container.

We cannot keep house like our grandmothers did because we don't have thirty hours a week to clean. Bursting. We cannot manage time the same way our mothers did when we live apart from our extended families in a world where community has been devalued. Bursting. We cannot cultivate marriage in the same ways when our husbands work twenty hours more a week than our dads did. Bursting. Once we accept this, we can stretch as life fills *us* up.

It's a choice of expectations.

Where do you need to cut yourself some slack?

Jesus constantly brings newness that cannot be confined within the old forms. The temple gave way to the church. The old covenant was exchanged for the new. The high priest was replaced by the priesthood of the believer. Church morphs. Culture progresses. Evangelism takes new forms.

God is a God of Today.

History certainly matters. It's a testimony to God's majesty and a road map to His presence. We learn from those who've walked before us. But we are not called to identically imitate our predecessors, because our contexts are different. Let's take their courage, their faith, their work ethic and allow God to pay it forward into Today.

You are not your mother. I am not my grandmother. What is required of us is hugely different. Our children are growing up in a changed world. Our husbands face trials new to this decade. What worked thirty years ago pertained to old wine. What is dished out today is new wine. Whether it's better or worse is irrelevant. What matters is that we choose to be new wineskins, able to stretch.

Cheers to us.

Do you need to cast off old ideals that aren't appropriate anymore? Are you hung up on trying to be like your mom? Ask God to show you what must be tossed out.

Dancing Monkeys

Today we're going to lay the foundation for the rest of this study. Some tangible changes will follow, but it is all rooted in this one attitude.

Come with me, please, through a summary of women's roles via our stereotypical predecessor, Barbie. Oh sure, she's no Susan B. Anthony, but she's as good a barometer of our journey as any since her fashion-model debut in 1959. She was joined two years later by her beau, Ken, who Mattel recently disclosed was never actually married to Barbie. That makes her something of a tart, but let's not dwell there. In keeping with *The Dick Van Dyke Show* and the Cleavers, Barbie held down acceptable jobs like candy striper and ballerina. She was, of course, thrilled about it.

For Barbie, the 1970s were a confusing era. Women's lib was on the rise. Barbie readjusted, becoming a surgeon and an Olympic downhill skier. Glass ceiling, my eye. By the '80s, Barbie had her groove on. She was a hard-nosed business exec and UNICEF ambassador because she loved money *and* children. Progressive. She simultaneously maintained her sex appeal to Ken by excelling as an aerobics instructor.

The 1990s tested Barbie's will like never before. Seemingly, there were no doors left to open, so wide had they been flung. So in 1992, she ran for president wearing a red, white, and blue glitter gown. The spotlight can be unforgiving though, and talking Barbie was heard saying, "Math class is tough" that same year. How *did* she become a paleontologist and engineer? It was shameful. She made up for it by running in predominantly male circles for the remainder of the decade: as a police officer, pilot, marine, and NASCAR driver.

In 1998, Barbie fell on hard times. Her boobs shrank and her waist expanded. Ken still loved her, though she was a beached whale by comparison. To avoid scandal, Barbie's kids—Skipper, Tutti, Todd, Stacie, Kelly, and Krissy—were passed off as her siblings rather than as her and Ken's illegitimate children. Mattel said the two have officially split, so Barbie marched into the new millennium trendy as ever: single.[2]

In what ways do you feel like—or not at all like—Barbie?

Perhaps Barbie's worst assault, other than those chichis, is that darn smile. Wipe it off, or so help me, I'll rip your perky little head right off! To look at her—and on a broader scale, our culture—you'd think women should be acceptable (or was it radical?), invincible, sexy, impervious to insecurity, rich and benevolent, always happy, and never aging. Green is gold.

Death to Barbie.

Rather than chase impossible standards dictated by this unforgiving world, let's rise up, Girls, and declare that we won't be dancing monkeys anymore. As God promised, we can exchange our weariness for strength (Isaiah 40:31). This requires a journey. The Jews were set free from Babylon, but they had to walk eight hundred miles back to the Promised Land.

The rest of this study hinges on this day. We must answer the following question and prepare for a radical shift.

Monkey, who are you dancing for?

I'm sick of this conversation. We discuss this in every small group, we hear it from our pastors, and authors harp on it. This one attitude shift would change our lives, yet we won't do it. We dance for the approval of our mothers, our neighbors, our bosses, church people, magazines, *strangers*. We require their esteem. We beg them to validate us.

Believer, why?

Why?

Why?

What can they tell you that God hasn't already said? The dance draws us toward discontentment, identity crisis, and despair. Everyone else is judging me. Everyone else has more. Everyone else is better.

Everyone else.

Everyone else.

Who do you work so hard for?

What are you hoping to receive from them?

I'm desperate for women to stop performing. In *Searching for God Knows What*, Donald Miller asked,

> What if our value exists because God takes pleasure in us? I know this isn't a very Marlboro-man way to live your life [or a very Barbie way either] but what if the Marlboro-man way of life really sucks and makes you lonely all the time. . . . What if when we are with God . . . we feel His love for us and know . . . that we matter? I feel like I am in a lifeboat trying to get other people to say I am important and valued, and even

when they do, it feels as though their opinion isn't strong enough.[3]

Around 870 BC, God inflicted a crushing drought on Israel to make her turn back to Him. After three and a half years, God sent Elijah to deliver His word to King Ahab, and a contest emerged. Elijah represented devotion to God, while Israel bowed to Baal under Ahab's leadership. Courageously, Elijah faced them all.

Read 1 Kings 18:16-19. How did Ahab misinterpret the trouble Israel was enduring? What was the truth?

Believer, we are quick to point fingers, too. "I'm forced to keep up." "Everyone puts so much pressure on me." "I didn't ask for all this stress." Yet by our performance, we choose our audience. In bowing to expectations and running around like medicated chickens to appease the opinions of others, we perpetuate the cycle. We *fuel* the cycle. We've brought trouble on ourselves.

Can you change the media? Can you silence the expectations of culture? Can you level the playing field of accomplishments or possessions? Of course not. And you'll never arrive, because someone will always be further along than you. The only thing you can control is who you dance for. Either perform for a merciless audience of humanity, or dance for an audience of One. There is no middle stage.

Choose.

Read 1 Kings 18:20-21. Why do you think the Hebrews had a hard time choosing between God and Baal?

*Do you have a specific role in which you're choosing worldly opinions over God's? Explain.

Get this: The Hebrew word for *waver* in verse 21 is *dance*. How long will you dance between two opinions? How long, Believer? Forever? Will you go to the grave never knowing your own value? Will you just keep working harder? A feverish dance is bound to attract applause eventually.

How long will you parent to please your mother or mother-in-law? How long will you carry bitterness because your husband's applause isn't loud enough? How long will you remain stagnant at church waiting for other believers to curtsy to your needs? How long will your friendships be poisoned by competition? How long will you exhaust your children so they'll reflect favorably on you?

Are you as tired from dancing as I am?

Read 1 Kings 18:22-29. What parallels do you see between the futility of this dance and the one you and I get trapped in? List everything you see.

This devastates me. These were God's people, His special treasure. He raised them up from Abraham, brought them out of Egyptian captivity, blessed them through David and Solomon. And here He saw them dancing like monkeys for a god that didn't exist, exhausted, drenched in their own sweat and blood, hoarse from screaming for validation *that would never come*. God's heart ached with grief, as it does today when we engage in the same futile dance.

*Read 1 Kings 18:30-39. What is God showing you about our dance?

Many feel God's holy fire couldn't affect us, so drenched are we. We're drowning in anger, bitterness, frustration, false expectations. Keeping up has so overwhelmed us, it seems we're beyond God's help. Oh, Believer, hear Elijah's sweet words: "Answer me, O LORD, answer me, so these people will

know that you, O LORD, are God, and that *you are turning their hearts back again*" (verse 37). God's holy demonstration wasn't to shame them. It was to give them a new audience who would delight in them.

God never asked for dancing monkeys.

It is time to stop performing for mankind. It's a burden we can't carry if we want peace, joy, security. We must relinquish this compulsion if we want passionate marriages and healthy children. This weight will overwhelm godly friendships and fulfilling careers, too.

Today is the day.

After God's holy fire, Elijah told King Ahab, "Go, eat and drink, for there is the sound of a heavy rain" (verse 41). Believer, the drought can be over. Lift your eyes to heaven and let God's rain pour down. Let it rain. Tilt your face toward God and let it rain. Get off the stage of humanity and let it rain. Quit wasting your life trying to measure up and let it rain. Stop the feverish dance and let it rain. Discover that your value exists because God takes pleasure in you and let it rain.

Let it rain.

"I will build you up again
    and you will be rebuilt, O Virgin Israel.
Again you will take up your tambourines
    and go out to dance with the joyful."
        (Jeremiah 31:4)

Who do you dance for? Ask God to show you all the places you're waiting for applause. Pray for strength to exchange your audience.

Curses

At this point, you might feel something stirring. Once we face the futile dance for humanity, we see it for what it is: worthless; exhausting; never over. It doesn't give back. Yet you may be tempted to change your audience but continue the dance of appeasement. "I'm not working to please others anymore. I'm working only to please God."

Believer, may I lovingly say you'll end up in the same spot you just tried to leave. Oh sure, it might take longer to feel the strains, and you'll start with more enthusiasm, but soon you'll be covered in sweat wondering why you're so tired. Doesn't God see me? Isn't He happy with all I'm doing for Him? Why do I feel empty? The authors of *TrueFaced* wrote of this shift:

> Something happened to many of us in the intervening years. We lost confidence that his delight *of* us and new life *in* us would be a strong enough impetus for a growth that would glorify God and fix our junk. So, we gradually bought the slick sales pitch that told us we would need to find something more. . . . Something magical and mystical that we would receive if we tried

hard enough and proved good enough, often enough. And so we . . . went back to trying to impress God and others—back to posturing, positioning, manipulating, trying to appear better than who we were. Our two-faced life has severely stunted our growth. And broken our hearts. And left us gasping.[4]

How do you feel standing before God today? What do you think He's thinking of you?

The Enemy has us so confused about grace that we actually believe that God's pleasure in us is based on what we do for Him. Satan twists the knife when we mess up, because then God is disappointed. Our relationship is conditional on our behavior. So if we just keep trying harder and sinning less, we will be godly and Jesus will finally be happy.

As a result, our relationship with God is void of authenticity. Rather than producing joy and maturity, it highlights our deficiencies and deepens our self-loathing. We falsely characterize God as harsh, impossible to please, chronically disappointed in us. Though our outer appearance says otherwise, our inner lives are broken because we can't seem to get (or stay) on God's good side. It would be better to be lost than to always feel like a failure.

Read Galatians 3:1-3. Oh my land. What trap had the Galatians fallen into?

*Believer, read it again. Why do we accept grace for salvation but deem it insufficient for the rest of life?

Girls, we can't go on without embracing this. Not another day. We often read Scripture like this and blame legalism. Well, they said it had to be this way and couldn't be that way and

puffed themselves up over the whole thing. Shame on them. Pride comes before the fall and all that.

Yet the same principle applies when we try and try and fail miserably. Legalism swings both ways. For the uber-exceptional, following the law breeds judgment. But for the rest of us, it breeds despair. Which is worse? Can't you hear Paul's desperation? Are you now trying to attain your goal by human effort? When we think it's good enough, it's not. When we think it's not enough, we're right. So is this spiritual experiment a big fat waste of time? Will we live, fail, and die?

Read Galatians 3:4-5. How do you answer Paul's questions here?

Martin Luther launched the Reformation in the 1500s through this teaching. Galatians was called "Luther's book" because he embraced this freedom to release believers from their self-imposed bondage to God. When asked about his neglect of pilgrimages, fasts, and other forms of standard piety, Luther said,

> If you are a preacher of mercy, do not preach an imaginary but the true mercy. If the mercy is true, you must therefore bear the true, not an imaginary sin. God does not save those who are only imaginary sinners. Be a sinner and let your sins be strong, but let your trust in Christ be stronger, and rejoice in Christ who is the victor over sin, death, and the world.[5]

You'll discover where you fall by how you're receiving this. Do you feel relieved? Skeptical? Even angry? Believer, pride convinces us we are good enough and everyone else isn't trying hard enough. But did God give us His Spirit and work miracles among us because we observe the law or because we

believe what we've heard about Him? Do we please Him with our trust or our efforts?

🔊 *Read Galatians 3:10-14. What can we expect by living out of our efforts? List everything you see.

Does that sound familiar? What an agonizing way to exist. How discouraging! So Jesus became the curse we couldn't escape by ourselves. The curse of striving but not achieving. The curse of trying to be holy but blowing it. The curse of not doing enough. The curse of not being enough. The curse of the dance.

Believer, you are free from it.

You can stop trying to win God over. You don't have to worry anymore that He is disappointed in you. You can stop trying to get yourself holy, because Jesus made you holy the day He hung on the cross and became a curse for you. Can you receive that?

Donald Miller wrote, "To a culture that believes they 'go to heaven' based on whether or not they are morally pure, or that they understand some theological ideas, or that they are very spiritual, Jesus is completely unnecessary. At best, He is an afterthought, a technicality by which we become morally pure, or a subject of which we know."[6]

That sounds familiar. Paul wrote in Galatians 2:21, "I do not set aside the grace of God, for if righteousness could be gained through the law, Christ died for nothing!" If you are spinning your wheels for God, Christ died for nothing. If you control the level of affection God feels for you, Christ died for nothing. If you are responsible for fixing your sin, Christ died for nothing. If you prefer the chains of obligation over unearned freedom, Christ died for nothing.

Read Galatians 5:1-2. How did Paul characterize our defense against this attack? Lovey-dovey peace? Guitars and "Kumbaya"?

Girls, let's walk out of the Room of Good Intentions into the Room of Grace. As the authors of *TrueFaced* wrote, "The first room creates a works-based, performance-driven relationship with God and puts the responsibility on our resources. The second room places the responsibility on the resources of God. . . . God wants you to believe that he has already changed you so that he can get on with the process of maturing you into who you already are."[7]

If you are searching for verses about working and pleasing God (busted!), yes, they exist. But God and His writers assumed we were already *living in grace*. It's ludicrous that we'd prefer a merit-based relationship after Jesus redeemed us from that curse. You can hear the shock in Paul's writings.

Pleasing God comes after grace, not before. Not one solitary second before. If that's you, just stop working. You're better off doing nothing than trying to earn your grace. Crack open a few beers and be done with it; might as well enjoy your misery as best you can. Then at least you can quit feeling like a failure. Every dance performed to win God over is wasted.

*Why do you work for God?

Every dance offered because God's freedom sends you twirling is received with laughter. You dance because you're free, not because you need to appease. You work out your salvation because you're aware of His pleasure in you regardless. You, stripped of your works, are God's delight. He couldn't love you one ounce more than He loves you right this second. You'll never be more righteous than you are today. Not one

thing you could do or stop doing would change Jesus' mind about hanging on that cross for you.

Believe it.

Stop dancing until you believe it.

Begin a new dance once you do.

Ask God to pierce the layers you've formed around the lie of earning His affection. Open your hands. Release your efforts. Pray for scary, unearned grace.

Refresh

On the fifth day of each week, you'll spend some quality time in God's Word. It's a chance for the Holy Spirit to be your Teacher. Every teacher called to champion Scripture is but a dim reflection of the adventure that awaits you in the Word with Him. No one has taught me like the Spirit.

I'd love to show you how to ask healthy questions of Scripture, so I'll include some prompts. But these are not a list of questions to answer. They are helps for interacting with the Word beyond "What does this mean?" Use one or two or none. Let the Spirit lead to what He wants to show you. Great Bible study is not about having all the answers but asking the right questions.

I am a fan of journaling. Don't groan. You took notes in class (1) so you could record what you heard, (2) so you could look back later, and (3) because you cared what the teacher was saying. Use bullet points. Write fragmented sentences. God doesn't care. This isn't a novel, but journaling tells God, "I'm listening. I care what You're saying. I'm working through it with You." This allows the Holy Spirit to deepen your insight because writing requires you to consider Scripture longer than

the five seconds it took to read it. It is the gift of time.

Before you begin reading, spend time in prayer with the Spirit. Ask Him to teach you. Pray that He'll remove your preconceived ideas and show you truth. Ask Him to speak clearly.

Read Galatians 5:1-6 without pausing. Then go back and work through each section as the following outline guides.

Read Galatians 5:1.

- What did Jesus come to set us free from? What was it like before He came?
- What does it look like to stand firm for your own freedom? How might you take this stance in your various roles?
- *Burdened* means "to be caught or entangled in." How does this happen with our efforts as mothers, wives, friends, and so on?

Read Galatians 5:2.

- Circumcision was an outward act of religiosity in those times. The Jews judged anyone who did otherwise. How are similar arguments being played out today? What actions are you pressured into to gain God's acceptance?
- How does spiritual peer pressure influence your role as a mom? As a wife? What have you been told will please God more than what you're doing?
- Why is Christ of no value to those of us who live to please?

Read Galatians 5:3-4.

- Submission to the law cannot be selective. If you are chained to one part, you're chained to it all. Why is this a yoke of slavery?
- Paul said, "You who are trying. . . ." Are you trying so hard, Believer? Who are you trying for? What are you hoping to get back?
- As you work endlessly in your roles—even for God— do you feel alienated from Christ? Why does He seem far away when you're trying so hard?
- What does it mean to have "fallen away from grace"?

Read Galatians 5:5-6.

- Paul said we *await* righteousness. Does your works mentality cringe at the idea of waiting for God, trusting Him to do a wondrous work in you? Why?
- If we don't earn our righteousness by being a good wife, mom, believer, and so on, how do we get it?
- Jesus didn't care about circumcision. *But it was once such a big deal.* What else might have no value to Jesus, though you thought it did?
- If faith is all that counts, how are you doing? Do you believe God values you outside your work? Do you believe He doesn't need to change you but needs only to mature you into who you already are?

Girls, we can't talk about our roles until we get this straight. What good is a discussion on serving God if you think it's to earn His favor? How can you become the wife God intended if it's only to impress your church friends? How quickly will

the well run dry for you as a mother when you can't accomplish everything the books say? Working out of obligation is the last thing God ever wanted for us. It was for freedom that Christ has set us free.

Hear this: You are treasured. Not because you build self-esteem into your kids or you give your husband sex every time he wants it. Not because you are on four church committees. Not because you have an excellent work ethic. Not because you bring coffee to your friends and watch their kids. You are treasured because God loves you.

He will stand with you as you face all your roles. God knows how hard they are for you. You aren't alone. Your successes and failures as a woman don't dictate His feelings toward you. Get that straight. Quit living to please others. Quit living to appease God.

Just live in freedom.

The rest will come after that, not before.

Neither circumcision nor uncircumcision means anything; what counts is a new creation. Peace and mercy to all who follow this rule. (Galatians 6:15-16)

WEEK TWO

Believer

(HANNAH)

Beloved Party Pooper

My kids consistently exemplify marginal faith, God love 'em. Now, to be fair, they are three, five, and seven, so let's not cast stones yet. But they might represent the human condition best, frankly. My oldest son recently declared, "I love Jesus every single day!" Firstborn equals pleaser. To that, my daughter thoughtfully countered, "I love God on Sundays and Tuesdays."

Then last week we were teaching our kids about tithing. My youngest, Caleb, had three dollars, so I drew out thirty cents and talked about giving back to God. Caleb snatched his coins and screamed, "I don't want to give my money to God! I want to be richer than God!" He ran upstairs, and we haven't seen that money since.

The selfishness continued that night during prayer, as I led him toward reconsidering tithing. "Do you have anything you'd like to tell God?" I asked. Caleb nodded (resolving it, I thought) and prayed, "Dear God, please stop making barbeque sauce. It burns my tongue. Amen." That one's going to the penitentiary or the pulpit.

Don't we feel like them? Sure, we put an adult spin on it, but most of us have asked, "What do you want from me, God? Sheesh!" Seriously, what does He want? What does a healthy believer look like? We must discuss this first because when this role is out of whack, so is everything else. After our Bible study group took a short break, my Girlfriend Christi told us, "I have to have this. I need the Word. I don't like me apart from God."

Preach it, sister. Apart from God's presence, I'm the wife my hubby stays at work to avoid. Separated from the Spirit's living current, my kids say things like, "You're scaring me, Mommy!" My girlfriends worry about me. My job becomes a burden, not a pleasure. The whole house of cards comes crashing down.

So what is God's first order of business for you? As you rub your proactive hands together, what tasks do you expect Him to assign to you? Be holy? Serve the church? Take care of others? Get that sin patched up? God's first priority for His daughters is this:

Be whole.

No, I mean, what do I do?

Be healed.

Yes, but what work do I do for You?

Let Me love you.

To you, is God a taskmaster or a father? Something else? How would you characterize your relationship?

We're walking with Hannah this week. In the Bible time-line, the major players went like this (with approximate dates):

Adam and Eve	A real long time ago
Noah	A little more recent
Abraham	2100 BC
(Egyptian captivity)	1875–1445 BC
Moses/Joshua	1500–1400 BC
Samuel, born to Hannah	1100 BC

David, Solomon, and most of the prophets will come later. There was no monarchy yet. Israel had been ruled by judges since Joshua led the exiles into the Promised Land around 1400 BC.

Joshua set up the tabernacle in Shiloh. The tabernacle was a large tent where the people gathered to worship God before Solomon built the permanent temple in Jerusalem. The Israelite men journeyed to Shiloh three times a year—the women once—to celebrate God at the tabernacle.

Now, when I say celebrate, I mean it. God was basically throwing parties. He was delighted to have His people safe in the Promised Land, free from bondage, secure under the Law He established through Moses. Captivity was behind them. Hundreds of years of work had come to fruition.

Read Deuteronomy 16:9–15. What atmosphere did God establish for these feasts?

The Old Testament God I once thought I knew might have said, "Be somber. Be sober. Be scared of Me, actually. Come to Shiloh and be very quiet and reverent. And wipe that stupid smile off your face, or I'll strike you with leprosy." We don't see that at all, but isn't that how we often think of Him? Or how we thought He was in the dusty days of ancient Israel?

But that's not our God.

He told His people to celebrate with joy. This was a time to laugh, rejoice, be happy, be blessed. They ate until they were

sick. They drank lots of wine. Everyone was back together in one place. The widows and fatherless looked forward to these feasts as the highlights of their year. The children anticipated them for weeks. The servants dropped their work and joined the festivities. These were happy, happy occasions.

For most of them.

*Read 1 Samuel 1:1-2. Hannah was infertile. Do you have a heartache that overrides other areas of happiness? Abuse? A broken marriage? A child in trouble? Shame? Poor body image? What is it, or what was it in the past?

Read 1 Samuel 1:3-8. How did the Enemy infiltrate this marriage to worsen Hannah's grief? List everything you see. (See Genesis 2:23-24 for a hint.)

Hannah and Peninnah probably lived in separate tents throughout the year. Their daily contact was limited. Unfortunately, the whole dysfunctional crew journeyed together to Shiloh. Can't you hear Peninnah? "Wow, children! Look at all our meat! There are just so many of us. We can eat three cows. Oh, are you still here, Hannah? What a cute little portion of meat Elky gave you by yourself. If that's not enough, you can have all my sons' leftovers."

Meanwhile, Elkanah couldn't understand why his love wasn't sufficient and called Hannah out on her despair. All this during a happy feast when God required this heart condition: "I have not eaten any of the sacred portion while I was in mourning" (Deuteronomy 26:14).

Have you ever felt as if God and everyone was saying you should be happy when your heart was breaking? What was it like for you?

We've messed this up something terrible. Faith has become

a juggling act of good behavior, measurable deeds, a chipper attitude. We've projected our notion of godliness onto the broken, rubbing salt into their wounds.

"Why are you still sad?"
"Why can't you get over this?"
"Immerse yourself in the work of the church."
"Put on a happy face."

So most of them do. But they're still broken inside. And that, Friends, is a cross section of our churches, an elaborate masquerade with complicated choreography. We hand out lists of appropriate behaviors—volunteer here, attend this and that, read this book, and, for heaven's sake, fix that sin of yours—but it's all useless. A broken heart cannot be mended by serving in the church nursery.

*Read Isaiah 28:10-13. My stars! This could've been written yesterday. According to God, where have we gone wrong?

What is God's tone here? What can you pick up on in His heart?

God doesn't want you to suffocate your heartache in favor of His busywork any more than you want your daughter to fetch her own dinner with two broken legs. Can you hear His urgency in Isaiah? "This is the resting place"! "Let the weary rest"! Resignedly punching out line items to appease God does nothing but break His heart.

Believer, God wants wholeness for you first and foremost. If you are injured, bench yourself and rest in the care of the Healer. Playing church while wounded not only compromises the team but also delays healing, making the injury far worse.

It is lunacy to think God would ignore your brokenness and prefer your sacrifices at the risk of your spiritual health.

Are you playing church while injured? If so, why won't you allow yourself to rest and heal?

Hannah didn't take part in the feast, even though God said, "Come, eat and be merry!" She didn't force down one bite, though everyone else was having a grand old time. In transparency, she sat at the table and wept. She refused to put on the happy God-face and play nice. Rather than please everyone else, she let her grief be real. How they handled it was not her problem.

And God didn't care about her untouched dinner.

He cared only about her sadness.

*Are you real with your sorrow? Why or why not?

How do the expectations of other believers play into your answer?

Believer, I beg you, choose authenticity over appropriateness. Risk inviting other believers into your struggles. You'll find more compassion than you could have hoped for. An honest community breeds more honesty. One girl drops her mask, and five others follow suit.

It is always worse to suffer in darkness. The Enemy convinces us to hide, but the fruits of darkness are shame and isolation. When heartache is brought into the light, it loses some of its power over you. Plus, it's attacked tenfold when other believers join your fight. The truth *will* set you free. This is what God wants for you, and He doesn't ask for obligatory service before then.

Service should come from a mended heart, a heart that's

been loved to wholeness. A heart that can look back and say,
"See where God has brought me." That's the only service He
asks for. It's birthed out of gratitude, not compulsion.

And wait until you see how He can get you there.

Are you faking it? Pray for courage to be real. Ask the
Spirit to empower you to rest. And if you're in a
healthy place, ask God to reveal a broken believer near you.
Pray for an opportunity to show her authentic love.

An Honest Mess

I have an interesting dichotomy in my life, demonstrated in my closet. On one side, I have cuffed wool pants, trendy little jackets, boots I asked forgiveness rather than permission for. You'd look at that side and think, *This girl just may have it together.* (False.) But on the other side of those clothes are a myriad of drawstring capris, faded jeans, and no less than thirty T-shirts. Next to the sticker-shock boots are fifteen pairs of flip-flops.

One side represents the times I'm a speaker. I wear makeup, use a lot of hair product, and spend time with people I don't know. Now, I love this. Teaching brings life to me like oxygen, but my conversations sound like a first date. "And what do you do? And how many children do you have?" That is the polished me, the "on" me. I still fly close to the surface, but my frank personality scares strangers, so I rein it in a bit.

The other side is the real me. The me who wears a ponytail so often that no one knows how long my hair is. This me wears jeans and T-shirts and sits with my girlfriends for hours. I get to be neurotic or obnoxious or terrified. We talk about *American Idol* without fearing ridicule. Any of us could burst out crying at any moment, and we'd call that normal. If I had to choose

one half of my closet over the other, someone at Goodwill would be ecstatic to find those boots for five dollars.

Relationship. Life without it is meaningless. We crave it from the first moment we breathe. We want to be known and loved more than anything else on the planet. It trumps success, money, power, knowledge. It has been the true measure of richness since there was life to measure.

This is how God wants to do life with us.

Donald Miller wrote, "I think it is more safe and more beautiful and more true to believe that when a person dies he will go and be with God because, on earth, he had . . . a relational encounter with God not unlike meeting a friend or a lover or having a father or taking a bride. . . . I believe the Bible is screaming this idea and is completely silent on any other, including our formulas and bullet points."[1]

Why do you suppose many prefer theology, denominations, or formulas about God over a real relationship with Him?

When we meet Hannah, the Hebrews had been living in the Promised Land for about three hundred years. The generations who witnessed God's deliverance were gone. Their children abandoned the faith of their parents and became sitting ducks for idolatry. The final verse of Judges demonstrates the spiritual chaos: "In those days Israel had no king; everyone did as he saw fit" (21:25). They'd neglected their heritage and filled their minds with Baal worship.

To make matters worse, the inmates were running the asylum at Shiloh. Eli the priest's two sons, Hophni and Phinehas, were making a mockery of the tabernacle. They prostituted the priesthood, using it for financial and sexual gain, and turned away much of the faithful remnant with their disgusting lifestyles. And Eli was a shining example of how

not to parent. It was a travesty, and God's voice went silent (1 Samuel 3:1). To have His treasured nation turn away on the heels of deliverance was a dagger we'll never understand.

Read 1 Samuel 1:9-11. Given the national rebellion, why do you think God began this story with a beautiful faith like Hannah's?

Hannah has some excellent lessons to teach us, Girls, as we ask, "What do you want from me, God?" Look at verse 10 again. The NASB says Hannah "wept bitterly," meaning *to weep in grief*.[2] Don't mistake her for an angry, toxic woman scorned. That's a different bitterness God begs us to resist, so cancerous are the effects. Hannah's bitterness is the type of sobbing that cannot be contained. When your grief is so overwhelming, you fear it may kill you.

But don't miss it: She felt full grief, wailed facedown, *and* turned to God. Both/and. Believer, God does not want your good behavior but your honesty. He is real, not some plastic, heartless taskmaster ambivalent to your anguish. He'd take your messiest, ugliest prayer over your silence. Are you freaking out? He can handle it. Are you angry and confused? He already knows that. But God is a parent; He'll walk through the flames with you. You are His daughter, not His nameless subject.

Read 1 Samuel 1:12-16. Why do we often misunderstand the grief of other believers?

*How do these misunderstandings make it hard to live honestly?

Girls, God wanted a relationship with Hannah, and nothing less would suffice. She didn't participate in the feast. Big deal. She cried during the whole dinner. So what? She chose

time with God over false sacrifices. Now we're on to something. As we search out balance in our roles, hear this: God would rather you *know Him* than anything else.

Believer, God wants you. The real you. Jesus did not die so we could have a new set of rules. God wants your heart!

Are you trying to please anyone with your God work? If so, whom?

*Forget the stuff you do. How is your relationship with God? Who is He to you?

Girls, God would have you forsake every task you perform *for* Him in favor of time well spent *with* Him. If your faith looks more like a to-do list than a friendship, you have derailed. Believer, give God what He really wants: time with you. Sit with Him and talk. Ask the Holy Spirit to journey with you through the Word. Be quiet and let God fill the space around you.

Jesus cared so much about real relationship that He said these scary words: "Many people will say to Me on that day, 'Lord, Lord, did we not preach in Your Name? Did we not put out demons in Your Name? Did we not do many powerful works in Your Name?' Then I will say to them in plain words, 'I never knew you'" (Matthew 7:22-23, NLV).

What does a good, churchgoing Christian woman look like in your mind? Busy? Church-committee driven? Bible savvy?

Do you give God time to really know you? Do you take time to really know Him? If so, when? If not, why?

When and where will you meet with Him each day?

Hannah chose time at God's feet over everything else. She stole away from family, responsibility, and obligation and poured out her soul to Him. Her grief was so flagrant that Eli thought she was drunk. But God thought she was beloved. See, real relationship with God is messy. It might make others uncomfortable or cause them to question your sincerity. But God will span the universe to meet the believer who is real. He'd take an honest mess over a pretty lie any day.

If you don't have time to get to know God, pull out of every temporary thing that's stealing His time. Not another thing we'll discuss will even compare to this priority. Believer, know and be known by your Father. Give Him some undivided attention every single day. God promised He would meet you more than halfway: "I will give them a heart to know me, that I am the LORD" (Jeremiah 24:7).

Do you need time with God apart from any agenda? Ask the Spirit to show you the state of your relationship, and pray for the desire to give Him time well spent with you.

Unclenched Jaws

My Girlfriend Gillian was telling me about her dog, Alabama. She is a silly, happy dog on nearly every front, but she has this one toy. It's a rubber rolled-up newspaper, and she loves it fiercely. So when you try to take it out of her mouth, Alabama turns into Cujo. When defending her newspaper, she forgets that Gillian loves her, feeds her, cleans up her poop, and lets her sleep in bed with her and her husband. She is only the enemy when trying to yank that toy out of Alabama's clenched jaws.

Here's the sad part: Gillian wanted to put a doggy treat in it and give it back, but that stubborn dog wouldn't let go for a second. It's as if she thought, *I'm a dog. I smell my own butt. All I have is this toy, and I'd run straight into the white doggy light rather than let you take it.*

Don't we clench our toys so tightly when God asks for them? "No! This is my favorite thing! I won't let go of it!" Doesn't God know how much we love it? Doesn't He understand how tightly we need to hold onto our dreams? Our security? Our fists are so squeezed around our favorite things that we've white-knuckled God half to death.

*Are you holding something you can't release to Him? A dream? A fear? A pain? A sin? A relationship? What are you afraid He'll do with it?

Hannah has shown us the way. She gave God everything He really wanted. First, she chose to be authentic over appropriate. Then she offered time at His feet rather than time at His table. Today we'll see how she opened her hands and rejected white-knuckle faith.

Read 1 Samuel 1:9-11 again. Hannah let her grief be real not just before the other Israelites but at God's own throne. The only place she allowed her pain to take her was to God's presence—not to anger, retaliation, resentment. Not to callousness, hardness, rebellion. Not to self-loathing, condemnation, shame. We see none of that. We only see her laying her deepest heartache at God's feet, knowing He alone could handle it.

Where does your pain usually take you?

Why is it hard to release your extreme heartaches to God?

We'll come back to that crazy promise she made, but I want to show you how fully Hannah opened her hands to God. As she offered her deepest need to God's care, Eli thought she'd been hitting the booze. Drunk Israelites did cavort around the tabernacle, and with Hannah's facedown posture and tears (if you've been around a drunk girl, you can understand Eli's mistake), Hannah looked like another wayward Hebrew.

Read 1 Samuel 1:15-19. Where do you see Hannah's open hands here?

Sometimes God is such a miracle. After we've systematically theologized Him to pieces and divided Him into lists and assigned all the rules, He gently pushes those aside and does

God things that cannot be explained.

How can you analyze a woman who was nearly dead with grief one minute and healed the next? Oh, well, she got what she wanted. No. There was no baby kicking in her stomach. Okay, but the priest promised she'd get that baby—he knew a Guy. Eli didn't even know what she was praying for. He just gave her good wishes and sent her on. Reconciliation? Peninnah was waiting to tease her back at the table. A little understanding? Elkanah thought she was being dramatic, and Eli thought she was drunk.

All she did was open her hands and release her pain—which was also her dream—to God's safekeeping, and "her face was no longer downcast." Believer, God is strong enough to absorb your heartache before it is resolved. He'll take your burden. Dreams can be so heavy. Girls, God works miracles. If He can part a sea and make the seabed dry, then He can supernaturally lift your head.

*Why is this process stunted when we won't open our hands? What happens during the tug-of-war?

It must have been hard for Hannah to let that dream go. She probably counted days and ate certain foods and did all the things women do when they want a baby. Verse 7 tells us "this went on year after year." She white-knuckled until she was too tired to hold on anymore. Then she opened her hands and gave her dream to God without trying to take it back, and her spirit was saved.

And do you know what that God of ours did? After she unclenched her jaw, He took Hannah's favorite toy, put the nicest treat in it, and gave it back. Don't you want to know a God who loves like that?

Read 1 Samuel 1:20. The name Samuel means, "God hears." What Samuel are you asking for right now?

How is the desire for your Samuel affecting your relationship with God?

Why does releasing our favorite toy matter more than other spiritual stuff? The thing about what you want most is that it takes up most of you. Your darkest pain affects you more than anything else. Your greatest fear plagues you all the time. Your largest dream requires all your focus. Your affected relationship demands your undivided attention. We give ourselves away, bit by bit, to the hope of our Samuels.

Girls, God wants your hope because He alone can fulfill it. It's not to snatch your dream away; God's dreams for you go well beyond your comprehension. Sweet Friend, God hears you. A believer who opens her hands before God, releasing the hope of her Samuel, stands empty-handed for only a moment. Because that same open hand is free to receive God's goodness as He hands it back.

"I wish I could change my childhood." *Release.*
"I want to be married." *Release.*
"This career is my dream." *Release.*
"He hurt me." *Release.*
"I want to fix my child." *Release.*
"I'm scared." *Release.*
"I want this so badly." *Release.*

If it's true that God is after our hearts, then you can see why this matters so much. It's not the toy. *It's the trust.* Like it did for Hannah, it's allowing what burns most inside you to drive you into the arms of your Savior. There is no safer place

for your passion. He will either stick a treat in the top and place it back into your open hands, or He will show the better way you couldn't see while you were white-knuckling. Either way, He'll save your spirit.

And your face will no longer be downcast.

Can you release that biggest thing? Ask the Spirit for courage to stand before God and open your hands. He wants your trust more than anything.

Fellowship

I could hardly sleep last night thinking about this day of study. Today we see the thing that God does, the thing that changes a woman. You know what I'm talking about? When He does such a work that everyone else looks on in amazement? This is Hannah. A woman changed from overwhelmed to overflowing.

Remember where she has gone: She chose to be real rather than right. She neglected the party to pray, choosing time *with* God over false sacrifices *for* God. And she released the hope of her Samuel to God's safekeeping. God took that dream, stuck a beautiful baby Samuel in it, and handed it back to His beloved daughter.

So isn't that the end of the story? Happily ever after and such?

Read again 1 Samuel 1:11. Darn. Have you ever promised God something in crisis that you wished later He would forget? What was it?

Land sakes, it's easier to make a vow than to keep one. And Hannah, gracious girl! Couldn't you have shot a little lower?

She made the Nazirite vow, meaning *separated* or *dedicated*, which promised that Samuel would not drink wine, cut his hair, go near a dead person, or be unclean, and which bound him to God's full-time service, usually for a specific time. Yet here Hannah says, "I will give him to the LORD for *all* the days of his life."

God's eyes search for those who will contend for His glory. He finds the heart that releases her dreams not just for gain but for God's own fame. Of course, many have offered the vow but neglected to keep it. "God, if you will do this one thing, then I will do such and such." Yet out of her awe at the Lord's tenderness, Hannah remembered God because He remembered her first (verses 11 and 19).

Read 1 Samuel 1:21-23. Why do you think Elkanah mentioned the Lord's word to Hannah? What uncertainty do you think he was demonstrating?

Oh, Believer, hear this again: God would have your heart over your sacrifices. Hannah skipped church for probably three years to care for her baby. She stayed home and nursed Samuel, watching him grow into a chubby toddler running around the tent. For a season, one role trumped the obligations of another, and the vow was delayed. Girls, be encouraged! God graciously allows one need to take center stage, sometimes to the neglect of "churchy responsibilities," because He's not after your work.

He's after your worship.

*Do you ever choose churchy work over rest because of what others might think? What are you afraid they'll say?

Is it God's reaction you fear? What are you afraid He'll say?

Hannah was home, but her heart still belonged to God. And though she was absent from Shiloh, she was present with God. No doubt there were many prayers offered during those three years with her little one. God received them from a tent as well as He would have from a tabernacle.

"Thank you, God. You remembered me."

Read 1 Samuel 1:24 and Numbers 15:8-10. Why do you think God had her bring an additional sacrifice to the tabernacle when she brought Samuel?

*If you offered your Samuel—or the dream of your Samuel—to God (whatever that biggest thing is), what else would you have to sacrifice? Control? A time frame? Fear? A relationship?

In those days, there were six acceptable offerings to bring to the altar: sin, guilt, ordination, burnt, grain, and fellowship. They served different purposes and required different elements. The first three were mandatory; the last three were voluntary. Now, as you look over that list, which is your favorite? No duh. It's the same as mine, of course, and the one Hannah was offering: fellowship. Let's pass on the sin and guilt business and go to the happy place.

Two ideas were included in this offering: peace and fellowship. Peace is from the Hebrew word *shalom*, meaning "peace or wholeness."[3] It was a voluntary act of thankfulness, the result of a special vow, or what was called a freewill offering. The fellowship offering was the only sacrifice of which the offerer might eat a part. She, in turn, shared a part with the priest who stood by her at the altar. All other offerings were burned entirely, consumed only by God.

Do you see that when God asks for our Samuels—our freewill offerings—what He really wants is our fellowship? He is saying, "Let me share your sacrifice with you." He doesn't yank

our offering out of our hands, appeased for a spell. Neither does He snatch our dreams and run in the opposite direction, leaving us there empty-handed. Believer, when you offer your Samuel, you stay right there in the Holy Place with God, your sacrifice lying between you, fellowship so thick you could cut it with a knife.

The purpose of the fellowship offering was to have a little dinner with God, enjoy each other. Share the love with the priest. That offering is received joyfully when it is given cheerfully. And God divinely works through that sacrifice, bringing wholeness to the woman who offers it. He wants us to give our treasures not so He can have them but because *there is communion there.*

 Have you ever shared a treasure with God? A child? A gift? A talent? A dream? How was there fellowship there?

Read 1 Samuel 1:25-28. What emotions would you expect to see in Hannah? What do you see?

Girls, this was service from a grateful heart. It was a free-will offering, not given under compulsion. Hannah and God had traveled a real journey together, and Hannah gave out of her overflow. We're finally getting around to "What do I do for God?" Maybe you thought this week would be a to-do list of work. Of course, there's been none of that. Serving God has been void of relationship for so long He wouldn't let me make any more lists.

Can't you hear it in Hannah? The separation trauma we'd expect to see is absent. She can barely contain herself as she reminds Eli of their first encounter. "Do you remember me, Eli? I lay on this floor sobbing, releasing the hope of this boy to my God. And look at him! He's beautiful, healthy. God remembered me."

Eli probably had to squint at first. She stood there a little rounder, eyes ablaze, full where she'd been empty. And it was from this place, and only this place, that she offered her service to the God who cared for her spirit. That offering was a fragrant aroma, born out of gratitude and saturated in fellowship.

Where do you currently serve God in the traditional sense? Do you volunteer somewhere? Lead something? What do you do?

*Do you experience fellowship or something less in your service to God? How does your real relationship with God tie into your answer?

If Hannah's sacrifice feels horrific, know this: God truly shared her offering with her. That sweet toddler became the catalyst by which the entire nation was revolutionized. Early on, Samuel was the recipient of God's voice, activated after decades of silence. Through his leadership, God intervened on Israel's behalf and gave the people victory over their enemies. Samuel championed repentance and reform. The monarchy was birthed through his hands, as he poured anointing oil first on the unworthy head of Saul and later on the blessed head of David.

By the leadership of her son, Hannah was a member of a holy nation once again. Her offering became a national treasure in the capable hands of God. See, God doesn't mismanage the dreams we give Him, nor does He withhold them from us. Hannah gave God her pain, and He gave her Samuel. She offered Him Samuel, and God granted her a legacy we're still talking about today.

So it is with God. We present a little; He gives much back. It's less of a give-and-take, and more of a give-and-give. And throughout this exchange, there is fellowship between God

and His beloved child, who serves Him not because she has to but because she is loved.

What can you offer God out of your overflow? A talent He has filled you with? A relationship He has blessed you with? Resources? Time? Where has God made you full?

If you're empty today, will you ask Him to fill you up while you rest? What keeps you from this request, if anything?

He fills us to capacity so He can wring out that goodness elsewhere. He fills me with His Word until I burst. He fills my Girlfriend Leslie with mercy, my Girlfriend Christi with a heart for worship, my Girlfriend Christina with compassion for the world. Our fullness is often birthed out of our greatest void, and He has to pour into us for a while, replenishing what was dry. But when we're bursting, He gently squeezes us and allows our overflow to nourish the people around us.

Believer, give God your grief and let Him turn it into a blessing. Offer Him that returned blessing and let Him use it for His glory. This is service the way God designed it. It is born out of relationship and rings with authenticity. It is fellowship. It is wholeness. It is union. It's the only way to really live.

Do you need to look at service differently? Ask God to show you where He is filling you or where He would like to. Find out what He'd have you do with that overflow.

Refresh

Girls, be so happy for Hannah. She visited Samuel every year, bringing him a robe sewn by her own hands. Samuel became treasured, beloved by the whole land, favored by God. He was the voice of a nation, the mentor to no less than King David. And God remembered Hannah: Each year "Eli would bless Elkanah and his wife, saying, 'May the LORD give you children by this woman to take the place of the one she prayed for and gave to the LORD'" (1 Samuel 2:20). And He did. She had three more sons and two daughters.

Let's walk through the prayer she delivered when she brought Samuel to Eli, leaving him for the remainder of his life.

Before you begin, spend a few minutes with the Holy Spirit. Ask Him to open your eyes to truth in the Word and to teach you. Pray He will show you what He wants you to see. Then open to 1 Samuel 2:1-10. Remember, the following are simply suggestions to elicit a response. Use one or two or none. Let your thoughts expand through journaling. This is not a list of questions to answer, but I encourage you to read them all to learn how to ask good questions of God's Word. That's what

great Bible study is founded upon.

Read 1 Samuel 2:1-2.

- Hannah's heart rejoiced the moment she put her baby in the hands of another. What does this tell you about real relationship with God?
- She delighted in God's deliverance. What did God deliver her from? What has He delivered you from?
- Hear it, Believer: "There is no one besides you." Can you say that to God? Why or why not?

Read 1 Samuel 2:3-5.

- So many reversals! Has God ever reversed your circumstances? High to low? Low to high? What was He doing?
- Why do you think humility matters so much?
- Again, God wants our hearts first, not our deeds (verse 3). Are you more works-driven or grace-driven? Can you pinpoint why?

Read 1 Samuel 2:6-8.

- Why does God use extremes so often? What do they produce?
- Believer, are you sitting in an ash heap? How did you get there? God *searches out* those in ashes so He might lift them out. Will you let Him?
- Hannah spoke prophetically of princes and thrones before there was even the idea of a king. What might God be preparing you for? How might your current circumstances play into your future?

Read 1 Samuel 2:9-10.

- The Hebrew root underlying "saints" in verse 9 is also used of "the faithful" in 2 Samuel 22:26, where the term describes both God and His people.[4] There is holy communion between God and the woman who loves Him. Do you experience that mutuality, that fellowship? Why or why not?
- Yes! "It is not by strength that one prevails." Believer, have you attempted self-reliance? Are you trying to strong-arm yourself to wholeness? What is God showing you today?
- Again Hannah prayed for the king, God's anointed. *Anointed by her own baby*. What could God do with your Samuel? How far might He be able to reach with your offering?

Girls, I pray if you've heard nothing else this week, you've heard "relationship." If I didn't help you with the practicalities of church attendance, volunteer work, tithing, or accountability, it's because if you live in grace-covered fellowship with God, those things will take care of themselves. By His design, works and obedience come after grace. They're natural. In communion with the Spirit, He douses us with discernment to know how to serve Him best.

But so many have put those things first and left grace out of it. It's why a believer can tithe, come to Bible study, sing in the choir, and work in the nursery and still have a bitter spirit that poisons all her relationships. It's why Christian leaders can preach from the pulpit while they sleep with their secretaries. Works without relationship are powerless, tools in the hands of the Enemy.

I beg you, discover grace first. Believe that God loves you

because you are worthy of it. Jesus already paid for your new identity. The authors of *TrueFaced* explain God's thoughts like this: "What if I tell them I love them, will always love them? That I love them right now, no matter what they've done, as much as I love my only Son? . . .What if I tell them there are no lists? . . . That they can stop being so formal, stiff, and jumpy around me? What if I tell them there is no secret agenda, no trapdoor?"[5]

Girls, if you can believe grace, if you can live there, you will please God more than you ever could through your sacrifices. *That* is what He wants from you.

WEEK THREE

Wife

(SHULAMITE WOMAN)

Roommates Are for College Girls

Note: I'll make many references to marriage this week, but please allow the Spirit to apply the information to your situation. If you're single, maybe you'll consider your current dating relationship or a previous marriage. Perhaps you'll look at relationship patterns or project toward future goals. We'll discuss many issues of male-female relationships, however the boundaries look for you. And if it's simply not applicable, allow the material to educate you and say "pass."

The year was 1992. The place was Oklahoma Baptist University. The characters were me—a silly freshman—and Brandon—a tall junior. Through many orchestrated accidents, this cute guy sure was around me a lot. I got my mail and there he was, though he'd just checked his empty mailbox. I got silverware and there he was, replacing his fork that for some reason could no longer pick up food. I'd be at church and there he was, visiting the same one—just like last week. When my friends started dropping his name, attempting subtlety, the bells finally went off. You see, I was slow. And I was dense. Brandon all but tackled me to get my attention.

Fast forward to a much more serious place in our relation-ship—like three weeks later—and I'd transformed from slow to lovesick. I was in love. Guns N' Roses ballads belonged to us. We wrote sappy letters, and I made some sort of love collage for Brandon to display. (I was feeling dramatic.) I remember a lot of making out. We were obsessed with each other, and being around us was pure saccharine. I'm sorry, Everybody Who Was There.

Girls, remember the early days with your guy? Pure affec-tion trumped the little things. Love won more than it lost. Sacrifices didn't extract grumbling. We rubbed their feet, for heaven's sake. If we could've bottled that affection and sprinkled it around later, sure, we'd be poorer and off task, but wouldn't we be a little happier, too?

This week we're looking at one of the hottest, steami-est relationships ever recorded: Solomon and the Shulamite woman in the Song of Songs. Whether you've been married for thirty years, you're divorced, or you're still dating around, we'll check places in our relationships with men that may be out of balance. This might be information for today, or maybe you'll sock it away for future reference. Either way, let's administer a little CPR to this role, breathe some new life back into it.

Affection is defined as "a tender feeling toward another; fondness."[1] On a scale from one to ten, how would you rank the affection level in your marriage? Does one partner get a higher score? Why did you answer as you did?

If you're uncomfortable with sex and passion, this will be a stretching week. But I beg you, stay with me. Discover that God is radically pro-sex, thrilled about heat between a man and his wife, even happier about their affection.

If you think God is apathetic about intimacy, you've

obviously never read Song of Songs. Most scholars attribute this love story to Solomon and read it as a beautiful poem about the courtship, marriage, and relationship between him and his bride.

PS: I don't think this is an allegory about God and His people. I don't think it's symbolic for Jesus' love for His church. I think it's about a guy and girl who can't keep their hands off each other. It's a perfect picture of what God wants for marriage. Listen, God didn't create our bodies and later exclaim, "Oh my land! Look what they can do together! Didn't see that one coming."

God called Himself *King of kings, Lord of lords, God of gods.* Solomon wrote 1,005 songs, but only this one is called *Song of Songs.* What does that communicate to you?

Read the words of Solomon's fiancée, referred to as Beloved or the Shulamite, in Song of Songs 1:1-4. What favorite elements of romance do you see here?

These two were starting a slow burn. They weren't married yet, and they refrained from sex until they were, but they were hot for each other. They desired each other physically and emotionally. Just the sound of his name was like incense, causing her to close her eyes and breathe him in deeply. And she didn't miss those glances other women cast at him. She had a catch; she knew it, they knew it, and she knew they knew. She had her eyes—and her lips—on the prize, and she was pining away for the bedroom.

This is where we all began. Nobody trudged apathetically through the early stages of love. None of us looked at our guy and said, "Well, I don't want to die an old maid, so let's just get on with it." No! We were smitten, attracted, obsessed even. We

saw wonderful things in our men. We were girls in love, and our guys probably never felt so desired.

*List the top five qualities you loved about your husband when you first fell in love.

Many say this stage of love is inferior to the later stages, and on some levels that's true. A mature relationship is deeper, well-worn with shared experiences, children, and longevity. But presuming desire should give way to comfort is malarkey. When I hear, "Love is not a feeling," it sounds cold, like we should abandon our need for affection, touch, passion that might get out of hand.

Many wives have tipped from affection to function. Our husbands are glorified roommates, and we share an address more than passion. You might be thinking, *But, Jen, my sexy boyfriend turned into a husband who dribbles pee on the toilet. My romantic date became a spouse who can't pick up his own underwear. Plus, he snores like my grandpa.*

Maybe your scales have tipped in a more tragic manner. You've been betrayed. Your husband struggles with porn. Perhaps he is abusive, verbally or physically. Maybe he is absent; he's home, but he's not. Sweet Friend, if your marriage has suffered a catastrophic blow, I beg you, seek Christian counseling. These injuries are beyond your boundaries. I know it would cost your pride, your controlled image to seek help, but is that worse than a destroyed marriage? A family in crisis? A lifetime of loneliness?

*If affection for your husband has given way to function, can you look deep and see where *you* are responsible? What have you allowed? How have you contributed?

Did you come into marriage with any inflated expectations? If so, what were they?

I'm not telling you to be a doormat Christian wife who should take all responsibility, letting your husband be the clod that he is. However, I haven't found the formula for controlling someone else's behavior. I'm still looking, of course, but until then, we can manage only ourselves. In *To Love, Honor, and Vacuum*, Sheila Wray Gregoire wrote, "Unless you have worked through what you are responsible for in your past and taken action to change yourself, you don't really know what your relationship can become."[2]

Let me ask you this: Who were *you* when your husband fell in love with you? How were you interesting? What attracted him to you? How did you care for your appearance? How did you treat him? What was it like to be around you? How were you exciting to him? What kinds of things did you say to him? Why did he want you for his wife?

How would you answer some of those questions?

What has gotten in the way since then?

God is into all this, you know. He talked about the early stages of love as far greater than the complacent later ones. In fact, He compared our feelings about Him to that same sad digression.

Read God's advice to the church in Ephesus in Revelation 2:4-5. If you apply that to the love you had initially for your husband, what is God suggesting?

Take your pick, Girls:

1. Remember that intoxicating affection you felt. Go there. Think about your husband as you once did. Reject any bitterness that has overshadowed those memories. If you insist on holding your anger, you can forget a happy marriage. Remember. See those qualities in the man standing before you.

2. Repent. Own the things that belong to you. It doesn't excuse your husband's behavior or render him innocent, but you're not responsible for him. Believer, own your anger or apathy. The way you deal with it is your responsibility. How have you contributed? Get honest with God. Swallow your pride and get honest with your husband.

3. Do the things you did at first. Fix your hair. Wear perfume. Talk sweet/sexy. Love your husband with your words. Initiate sex like you'll die without it. Be interesting again. Be that girl he couldn't resist. You're still her. Ask your husband what attracted him to you. That may be a real eye-opener.

*Do you see anything that needs to be done? If so, what?

Will you try? Why or why not?

If this seems like a lot of work and you're already tired, I'll lovingly remind you that a great marriage *is* a lot of work. There's no formula for making it easy. Complacency has never yielded a healthy union. And if it feels unfair that you're trying when your husband isn't, Believer, you're probably right.

You've been hurt or ignored or taken advantage of, and it's not fair.

Now may I ask you something? Is clinging to your rightness working for you? Is it producing a great marriage? Is it keeping you warm at night? Your Enemy would have you cling to your pride, convinced that you alone will guard it. He would also like to see your marriage shattered or the loneliest place on earth. He'd keep you isolated from your husband and spiraling in despair, desperately clutching your pride.

Believer, please choose your husband. Stand with Jesus and face your marriage together. Allow Him to activate affection that might be dormant. God loves marriage. If He can raise dead, dry bones into a living, vibrant army with one breath (Ezekiel 37), He can revive love until it becomes a feeling again.

Believer, go to the place of affection. Remember. Search the areas that have diluted the love you had at first. Pray for forgiveness, selflessness, pure love.

Two Winners

Housekeeping Monthly, May 13, 1955, offered tips for wives as they prepared for their husband's arrival home from work. The article was called "The Good Wife's Guide." Here's a taste of it:

- "Over the cooler months of the year you should prepare and light a fire for him to unwind by. . . . After all, catering for his comfort will provide you with immense personal satisfaction."
- "Prepare the children. Take a few minutes to wash the children's hands and faces, . . . comb their hair and, if necessary, change their clothes. They are little treasures and he would like to see them playing the part."
- "Minimize all noise. At the time of his arrival, eliminate all noise of the washer, dryer or vacuum. Try to encourage the children to be quiet."
- "Listen to him. You may have a dozen important things to tell him, but the moment of his arrival is not the time. Let him talk first—remember, his topics of conversation are more important than yours."

- "Make the evening his. Never complain if he comes home late or goes out to dinner, or other places of entertainment without you. Instead, try to understand his world of strain and pressure and his very real need to be at home and relax."
- "Don't complain if he's home late for dinner or even if he stays out all night. Count this as minor compared to what he might have gone through that day."
- "Arrange his pillow and offer to take off his shoes. Speak in a low, soothing and pleasant voice."
- "Don't ask him questions about his actions or question his judgment or integrity. Remember, he is the master of the house . . . You have no right to question him."
- "A good wife always knows her place."[3]

I'm thinking it was good to be a man in 1955. You know those wives spent their nights in the garage sniffing paint. Except maybe the rebels who brazenly ran the vacuum when the master arrived. Wicked girls.

A lot of church fellas really latched on to this back in the day. Why wouldn't they? They could stay out all night without answering for it and have their shoes removed by their servants . . . I mean wives. Add some misinterpretation about submission, and the relationship between a man and his wife got jacked up.

This is why God stuck the Song of Songs in the Bible. His plan never supported this insanity. Just like we've messed up stuff like humility and evangelism, we've distorted one of His favorite components of marriage (and all relationships, for that matter): mutuality.

Read Song of Songs 1:9–2:7. Pick one thing Beloved said about her lover. What was going on in her heart to say that?

Look specifically at something he said about her. What does it communicate about their relationship that he would say those words?

*How did you feel when reading this? Grateful? Jealous? Sad? Angry? Why do you answer like that?

Solomon never treated her condescendingly, heaping his comforts on the back of her subservience. Beloved never cowered, fearful of disturbing his space or infringing on his time. Nor did she nag him within an inch of his life until he acquiesced to her demands. That behavior would have ruined their relationship. Here we see beautiful mutuality that smacks of God's design. Neither partner is the winner at the expense of the other. They're both winners, securing love and respect from the other.

How is the mutuality in your marriage? Is one of you losing? Maybe both losing? Both winning? How so?

If you're losing, you can't control how your husband treats you or feels about you, though I'm sure you've tried. And you're right. Let that go. Nothing I'll suggest will be employed accurately if it's to manipulate your spouse. If you're out to change him rather than yourself, you will fail. Your resolve will lose steam the first time he disappoints you.

So what can you control? Yourself. This is a boundary issue, and it gets fuzzy for girls, but we must distinguish what is mine, what is his, and what is ours.

In what areas do you feel the scales are tipped, and you're losing? Taking care of the kids? The house? Emotional care? Respect? Sex? What else?

*Believer, look hard. How have you perpetuated the tipped scales in those areas?

Here's what I'm getting at: If it looks like a doormat, lies down like a doormat, and behaves like a doormat, it's always going to be one. No one knows to treat the doormat otherwise. She seems okay lying there and she doesn't try to get up, so I guess she belongs there.

This is not a battle cry for independence. God says we need each other desperately. Our souls were designed for intimacy. What's more, we're to serve each other as Christ did. But Sheila Wray Gregoire wrote,

> There is a marked difference between Christlike servanthood and the traditional subservient role of women. It is hard to properly serve as Christ did if you are regarded as inferior to those you are serving. . . . Subservience does not challenge people or aid them in understanding the character of God because the servant is doing only what he or she is expected to do.[4]

Have you allowed your husband to regard you as inferior? A good barometer is how your children treat you. If you're the subservient martyr, they'll pick up on it. Evaluate your position in the family.

Did you go to the opposite extreme, and you're the unyielding dictator? If so, where are you winning at your husband's expense?

*Either way, why have you allowed this? Are you trying to please someone? Are you buying into a faulty model of

marriage? Do you see yourself as inferior (or superior) to your husband? What else?

If your husband yells at you and your response is to try harder, why would he respect you? If he can watch TV while you cook dinner, clean up the kitchen, bathe the kids, help with homework, and engineer bedtime, why would he do otherwise? If you allow him to disrespect you in front of others, when would mutuality develop between you?

In *Boundaries*, Henry Cloud and John Townsend wrote, "Setting limits is an act of love in the marriage; by binding and limiting the evil, they protect the good. Taking responsibility for someone's anger, pouting, and disappointments by giving in to that person's demands or controlling behavior destroys love in a marriage."[5]

How you allow yourself to be treated, how you respond, and how long you engage in destructive confrontations are your choices. Your sole responsibility to your husband is to love him as he is today. Accept him and respect his choice to be that way, but set limits on being an enabler. That's the healthiest decision you can make for your marriage.

Boundaries are always about you, not the other person. Here are some examples:

Before Boundaries	*After Boundaries*
1. "Stop yelling at me!"	"You can yell, but I won't stand here while you do. I'll talk to you when you're calm."

Before Boundaries	After Boundaries
2. "Stop drinking! It's ruining our family. . . . You're wrecking our lives!"	"You can choose to deal with your drinking or not, but I won't expose myself and the kids to it anymore. The next time you are drunk, we're going to my mom's. . . . Your drinking is your choice. What I will put up with is mine."[6]
3. "I'm doing everything around here! Why won't you help? I'm sick of being a single mom!"	"You don't have to help, but I won't cook and clean up every night anymore. I'm feeling resentful, and that's my problem. There will be sandwich makings in the fridge, and we're switching to paper plates. Feel free to help yourself."
4. "Why do I always have to pick up all your stuff? I feel like I have another kid to take care of!"	"You can leave your things out, but I'm not going to put them away anymore. I'll put your things in a pile in the corner, and you can deal with them whenever you feel like it."
5. "You always make fun of me in front of other people! It's not funny to me! I hate it!"	"I've told you how I feel. I've brought my own keys, so the first time you disrespect me in front of someone else tonight, I'll leave."

Do you see the difference, Girls? When you do things for your husband that he should rightly do for himself, it's hard for him to respect you. Mutuality is short-circuited. Don't

mistake limits as a fancy way to control him. Yes, they might activate change, but only because that's how God designed responsibility. Enforcing healthy limits requires a partner to evaluate his behavior. If it's not paying off anymore, it might get red-flagged for change. But if it doesn't, you've still moved toward mutuality, and *that's a step closer to God's will for your marriage*.

Read Galatians 6:4-10. What was Paul saying about responsibility?

Do you need to set limits with your husband? Where?

If you're reaping what your husband is sowing, you'll burn out. Believer, set limits where they need to be set and then make a plan together. Decide what's yours—some things just are. I do the shopping, daily school maintenance, laundry, and most of the cooking. Decide what's his. Brandon does the yard, helps with school projects, finances, and handy work. Everything else we share: housecleaning, kids' activities, and, most importantly, *respect*. It rightly belongs to both of us. When the scales tip, we talk about it before going postal.

What's yours? What's his? What should belong to both of you? Get specific. Please talk to your hubby and decide together.

Resist the urge to compare yourself to anyone else or another family. This is about you. Are you trying to keep pace with someone else? Why?

This creates a manageable home. Life doesn't burden one more than the other. More importantly, it fosters a marriage of respect. Serving each other becomes what it should be: an act of love, not compulsion. Your husband wants you to have

self-respect. He'd rather be married to a woman of conviction than a doormat.

Be that woman, Friend. Give your husband a wife who respects herself as you do him. Free him up to love you, not use you. He wants to. Give him a partner worthy of esteem, and he will give just that. He will resonate with these words from Proverbs: "With great pride her husband says, 'There are many good women, but you are the best!'" (31:28-29, CEV).

Believer, ask for illumination on areas that are no longer mutual and pray for appropriate boundaries for you, not him. Put on self-respect because God made you worthy of it

Not on a Box, Not with a Fox

My Girlfriend Laura participated in a triathlon once. That's the most senseless thing to get worked up for, but this is clearly not my story. The race was here in Austin, Texas, on a record day when the temperature hit 108 degrees. That would've been my ticket to Baskin-Robbins, but again, Laura's story.

She'd gotten to the last part: running. Her body went ice cold, and she had tunnel vision. When she ran past her family one mile from the finish line, her husband jumped in with her because she looked like a Van Gogh painting. She started swerving like a drunk college girl and passed out on the curb. Laura spent the following hour in the infirmary tent for dumb, sick triathletes (again, I'm projecting my feelings here). She couldn't remember her own name, so she got a tickct to the ER, where she took in four bags of IV fluid.

Because I'm so merciful, I stated a fact: "You are an idiot." Listen, I'll quit jogging at the gym if they're not playing a TV show I like. I asked Laura why she didn't stop or make a smart girl's choice to walk. She looked at me like I was insane (though I've never required four bags of fluid to recall my own name).

"I was committed."

Indeed.

A strong commitment can see you through anything, except maybe lethal dehydration. Girls, let's look at the power of commitment and how it shapes our marriages.

Read Song of Songs 2:8-15. Why do you think Solomon preferred time with his Beloved on the mountainside rather than at her house? List everything you can think of.

Girls, sometimes we need to leave our homes that distract us, our kids who hog our attention, and our tasks that consume us and go to the mountainside with our husbands. If you think marriage should maintain intimacy on the merits of a vow once made, Believer, a vow is only words until it's actively fulfilled. A marriage will not self-propel. We must make time for our spouses. Not time at the table while our kids squawk for ketchup. Not time sitting at church. Not even time with friends.

Time alone.

What will you do? Sit with your husband and talk. Listen. Reconnect. Share honestly. Make out in your car. Take a walk. Take a trip. Have a picnic by the lake. Make a list of restaurants and conquer one at a time. Take a bottle of wine to the prettiest spot in town. Golf together. Drive through the country with your favorite music playing. Do what you like to do. Enjoy your husband and spend all your charms on him.

If it comes to paying a babysitter, it's worth the budget money. Maybe you trade kids with another couple twice a month. Beg your mother. Bribe your neighbor. Find a Parents' Night Out program. This is absolutely nonoptional. If you don't spend alone time with your husband, he'll turn into a roommate.

Do you spend alone time with your hubby? If so, when?

*If not, why? What is your biggest objection or obstacle?

Yesterday we discussed boundaries between you and your husband. Equally important are those you establish between your marriage and the rest of the world. The pressures, temptations, and opportunities available are endless. Many extras can disrupt marriage: work, kids, hobbies, interests, TV, in-laws, church, the Internet, friends. Most of those are fine things, but a couple's commitment comes first. When extras usurp that priority, they destroy intimacy, just like a third-party addiction or affair.

*Solomon referenced these extras in Song of Songs 2:15. What foxes sneak into your marriage to ruin it?

In *Boundaries in Marriage*, Cloud and Townsend wrote, "Most of us would like to avoid having to say no in life. . . . Yet reality dictates that in order to say yes to keeping a close marriage, you will have to say no to lots of other things. . . . You simply do not have the time, resources, or energy to do everything you want to do."[7]

We cannot have it all, and it doesn't feel fair. If 99 percent of your yesses are to your job and children, leaving 1 percent for your spouse, it will cost you. There is a lie that says you can give 100 percent to all these roles, but you can't. A devoted mother is little consolation to your children if they live in a war zone. A promotion won't hold hands with you after you're retired. Girls, you must clarify your life goals and ruthlessly prioritize toward those ends.

What are your goals for your marriage? Short-term? Long-term?

Have you said yes to something—good or bad—that has taken priority over your marriage goals? Maybe a life entirely revolved around your kids? Your job? How is it negatively affecting your relationship?

There is a balance between prioritizing your marriage and having a life outside it. Ruth Graham once said in an interview that her marriage to Billy was successful "because he plays golf, and I play bridge." Don't drop out of your book club and quit calling your mother; just evaluate those things honestly. Are they healthy? Are they a constant source of tension? Are they stealing your loyalty? Are they driving a wedge between you and your husband? If you don't know, ask your husband. Be willing to sacrifice for the sake of time with him. You'll never regret it.

Read Beloved's words in Song of Songs 2:16; 8:6-7. My stars! God put this right in His Word. How has He characterized marriage?

This doesn't happen just because you married a Christian. In fact, George Barna found that divorce rates are significantly higher among conservative Christians than any other faith group, including atheists and agnostics.[8] *The atheists are staying married more than we are.* Believers expect the mere presence of faith to protect their covenant. They neglect the armor of commitment, and the disillusionment leaves them reeling, giving up.

*Is this you? Did you come into marriage with rose-colored glasses on? Or did you come in so skeptical that you won't allow your marriage any bumps without declaring it a failure? Describe your situation.

Gregoire wrote, "Commitment to your husband is essential for any positive growth in your relationship. Until you can say, 'I am sticking with this marriage through thick and thin,' to a certain degree you will constantly be testing your husband."[9] Has he finally arrived? Is he good enough? Am I in this thing for real? This is a sandy foundation.

Do you need to nail this down once and for all? What, if anything, keeps you from sealing your promise?

Believer, commit. Put your husband like a seal over your heart. Write his name across your soul. This love can rival death in its strength; reject any substitute. Pray for a fire to rekindle your marriage. Look your husband in the eyes and choose him—with your time, your loyalty. The Spirit rushes into that kind of commitment and can ignite that flame into a raging inferno.

My lover is mine and I am his. (Song of Songs 2:16)

Ask the Spirit where the walls around your marriage have been breached. Ask God to temper your desire for the things that steal you away from your husband.

Hot Mama

My Girlfriend Christi was a virgin bride when she married her adorable husband. Now, when a church has browbeaten a girl with the dangers of sex throughout her entire adolescence, intimacy is nothing short of a terror. Christi was so nervous on her wedding night that she freaked out and pushed consummation back a day, God bless her.

The following night, she got her business together. She wore something provocative, lit some candles, and pulled out her ace: a sexy mix tape to create the mood. She propped her new husband up in bed while she set the stage. "Wait, wait, the candle went out! Hold on, my heels are snagging the carpet." Hollywood it was not. She finally closed her eyes and started channeling Marilyn Monroe. Christi swayed back and forth, doing a little come-hither dance, and pressed play on her mix tape.

And blaring from the stereo, they heard, "Oh Lord my God! When I in awesome wonder . . ." She'd accidentally grabbed a praise tape to seduce her husband with. Now, worship music is great, but it's an inferior sexual tool. It would've been less awkward had she invited her parents to the bedroom show.

Sex. Out of everyone I know, about three couples have

this sewn up. It seems God made an error or two. Men and women approach sex differently, think about it differently, need it differently, assess it differently. Yet we can get it only through each other. But God does not set us up for failure. So what was He thinking?

*How's the sexual vibe going for you and your husband? If you struggle, what is your biggest issue?

Think about the other facets of marriage God loves: affection, mutuality, and commitment. Girls, when those are flourishing, sex follows more naturally. God didn't drop us in the marriage pool and shout, "Spawn!" He placed the treasure of sex within marriage, fiercely guarded by emotional togetherness. When those layers are broken or absent, sex is vulnerable, void of the context in which it thrives.

That's how women see it.

Men see it reversed. When sex is broken or absent, the relationship is vulnerable, void of the sexual togetherness that allows it to thrive. Gregoire put it like this: "She makes love *because* she feels loved, and he makes love *to* feel loved. In other words, when she doesn't feel loved, the last thing she wants is to make love. But when he feels distant, the thing he wants most is to make love because that's how he fixes everything."[10] Houston, we have a problem. Let's see what we can learn from Solomon and his bride.

Read their wedding night pillow talk in Song of Songs 3:11–4:7. Try to get over the weird wording. How would you describe Solomon's assessment of his bride?

Shaunti Feldhahn wrote in *For Women Only*, "The effort you put into your appearance is extremely high on his priority list. Yet the chances that you know his true feelings are

extremely low."[11] It desperately matters to our husbands that we take care of our bodies and appearance.

This is complicated because it's such a hypersensitive issue. Imagine the verbal assault you'd unleash if he mentioned it: "Well, when you shove three babies under your stomach muscles until they stretch your skin like spandex, and nurse them on your boobs until they look like a pair of tube socks, then we'll talk. We'll just see how your butt responds to the *labors of childbirth*." It's a wonder they haven't brought it up. You'd better not either. He wants to say this as much as you want to hear it.

Feldhahn encourages us with this survey result: "Over and over again, I heard each man say that what mattered most to him was not that his wife shrank down to her honeymoon bikini, but that she was willing to *make the effort* to take care of herself for him." In fact, five out of six men emphatically agreed with that sentiment.[12]

How are you doing in this area? Do you try? Ever exercise? Sweatpants every day? Makeup on Sunday only? What do you look like to your husband on most days?

*How is this discussion making you feel?

Comparing yourself to other women will derail any progress here. Does the notion of measuring up paralyze you? Write your thoughts.

Dear Girlfriends, try not to be defensive. He's not shallow. It's how men are wired. Visual messages are hopelessly linked to his emotional center. Caring for your appearance makes him feel loved in the same way it affects you when he brings home flowers. When you value what he values, you communicate

your love for him. And for us, looking better leads to feeling better. Everyone wins.

🔊📻 Read Song of Songs 4:9-15. Beloved's got him panting. What sensual secrets can you borrow from her? Read closely.

She's a sexually powerful woman, certainly no shrinking violet. She was a locked garden until her vows; then she transformed into a garden fountain, a well of flowing water streaming down.

The church's urgent counsel against premarital sex ended up throwing the baby out with the bathwater. Listen, God is pro-sex. He's pro-sexy. Sister, you can be a tiger. In the married bedroom, you go girl. Wear it. Dab it on your neck. Say it. Pour two glasses. Be a little risky. Ruin his concentration the day after. You turn it on in the bedroom, and there's nothing your husband won't do for you.

🔊📻 Read Song of Songs 4:16–5:1. Is it hot in here? How is this exchange different from the obligatory "fine" we often give our husbands?

Who cares? Men just want sex, right? They don't care if we're into it. Wrong. In Feldhahn's survey, this topic earned the highest degree of unanimity: 97 percent of men said getting enough sex wasn't enough. Sheer quantity was not their desire. Rather, they needed to feel wanted. In fact, three out of four men said even if they were getting *all the sex they wanted*, they'd still feel empty if their wife wasn't both engaged and satisfied.[13]

Girls, we are relational creatures. We get emotional support from many sources. Most men live with a deep loneliness we don't understand. So often your husband stands alone—in the workplace, as a provider, and simply as a man,

independent and strong. For him, sex is the purest salve for that loneliness. In your arms he is accepted, desired, loved. When he knows you want him sexually, you are emotionally arming him to succeed everywhere else.

*What are you communicating to your husband in this area? Does he think you want him? If you don't know, ask him.

Finally, read the exchange between Solomon and his wife in Song of Songs 5:2-6. Sound familiar? What happened sexually here?

"I'm already asleep."
"I'm in my jammies."
"I've already showered."
"I'm exhausted."
"I've met needs since 6:00 a.m."
"If one more person gropes me, I'm getting the gun."
"I know that look, and you can forget it."

Girls, I know! Lord, have mercy, I understand. The idea of sex at 10:30 p.m. is so obnoxious sometimes that it makes us want to cry.

Sweet Friends, Solomon was hungry for his Beloved, but her rejection pushed him away until she couldn't even find him. He was reaching for her, needing her, and her dismissal was catastrophic. If your husband is distant today, maybe entirely lost, could it be he's been rejected for so long that he quit trying?

Remember, sex is not just sex to him. There is no stronger way to communicate your love to him than by your sexual desire. Inversely, there's no quicker way to verify his unworthiness than to reject him sexually. There is a tender heart behind

that testosterone, no matter how you think otherwise.

One husband said, "When she says no, I feel that I am REJECTED. 'No' is not no to sex—as she might feel. It is no to me as I am. And I am vulnerable as I ask or initiate. It's plain and simple rejection."[14] Believer, our husbands find us irresistible; they think about sex with us literally every hour. So when they feel unappealing to us, we don't understand how deep that cuts. You're thinking, *I'm just tired*. But he's hearing, *She doesn't want me.*

How often do you reject your husband sexually? Four out of five advances? More? Less? Would you bravely ask him how that makes him feel?

How much sex does your marriage need each week? Resist the urge to borrow another couple's number. One man's minimum is another man's exhaustion. This will require a conversation with your husband (one word: compromise).

Girls, we want the other pillars of marriage to be in place before dealing with this one. But it's only when sex is healthy that our husbands can meet our other needs. If all areas are dry, someone needs to be the hero. Yes, it's fair to feel entitled to mutuality and affection from him. But crippling his sexuality will never produce the kind of marriage you're dreaming of. Do you want to be right, or do you want to be happy?

Believer, be the hero. Run headlong into the intoxicating power of sex. Allow God to work supernaturally as you join physically with your husband. Let the Spirit use your gift to minister to your partner's heart, and you might be shocked how it changes your entire union.

God never wastes your offerings. He uses your forgiveness to heal relationships. He uses your testimony to minister to others. He uses your humility to lift you up.

And He uses your sexuality to impassion your marriage. God invites us,

Eat, O friends, and drink;
    drink your fill, O lovers. (Song of Songs 5:1)

Friend, will you pray over this issue? Ask God to heal you of resentment or wounds from your past. Pray for a radical desire for your husband to possess you.

DAY FIVE

Refresh

Not only will you study Scripture today, but you'll also have some marriage homework. Before you start, pray. Ask God to lessen your inhibitions. Pray for boldness to speak honestly to your husband.

It's interesting that the Song of Songs doesn't worry with talking about God. There's no Jesus stuff in there, no theological discussions. Solomon didn't present marriage religiously, void of emotion and tied with a churchy bow. God gave us this book as a beautiful portrayal of marriage, full of passion. God loves marriage. He wants this for you. He is very comfortable with the subject, and you should be, too.

Read the following passages and work through each question in your journal. I've asked you to put your thoughts into action. If you and your husband never talk about sex or your relationship, it's time you started. My Bible study group began talking frankly about marriage, and each week I said something like, "Go home and ask your husband _____." Several girls looked like I'd asked them to install a pole in their bedroom and do a striptease, but they mustered up the courage to talk.

By the end of that semester, our husbands bent over backward to make sure we never missed a Thursday night, so incredible were the fruits of our discussions. Don't underestimate the power of conversation. Trust me: Tell him, "I want to talk about our sex life," and he'll even turn off SportsCenter.

Read Song of Songs 5:9-16.

- List five words to describe Beloved's emotions toward Solomon.
- When is the last time you told your husband what you loved about him? How did he respond?
- Do you compliment him in front of others? My husband says this is even more important than building him up in private.
- What *do* you love about him? Physically? Emotionally? Spiritually? Take Beloved's emotions you listed and apply them to your husband.

Assignment: Plan an evening alone with your husband. Tell him what you love about him. If you're uncomfortable saying it, then write it. He wants to know he's attractive to you. (Drop some of these compliments in outside conversations in front of him. You have no idea how much he'll love this.)

Read Song of Songs 7:1-9.

- Verse 1:5 tells us her skin was dark, an undesirable quality then. She was no Heidi Klum, but she worked what she had. Believer, how is your body image right now?

- Is your body image interfering with your husband's pleasure in you? How so?
- Have you neglected your body? Have you let his favorite place go? You're not going to look eighteen again, nor does he expect you to, but how do you work what you have?

Assignment: Do not discuss this with him, but make a renewed effort to care for your appearance. Please don't mistake this for another idiot telling you to be a size 2. The Enemy would distract you with defensiveness. Will you show your husband your love by making an effort? You'll both be happy.

Read Song of Songs 7:9-13.

- Do you ever initiate sex? If so, how often? If not, why? My husband says this is the ultimate trump card, better than anything else I do sexually.
- Wine, sexy words, a night away, a little romp in the vineyard—lucky Solomon. What tools of seduction do you use? What could you try?
- Beloved said, "At our door is every delicacy, *both new and old*, that I have stored up for you, my lover" (verse 13). How's your game? Do you ever add any new tricks? Is sex with you exciting or always the same old thing? What's your heat factor in the bedroom?

Assignment: Read a book on sex; get some new tricks. I'm serious. Order it online if you're embarrassed. Ask your husband, "How do you think our sex life is going? What do you need from me sexually that you're not getting?" Before

the week is out, initiate sex. Try a new delicacy. You won't be sorry.

Girls, when our role as wife is rehabilitated, everything else is better. This discussion came second, after our relationship with God, because it's the most important earthly relationship we have. It is more important than motherhood because you do your kids a disservice when you sacrifice your marriage to make them the center of your universe. Give your kids the gift of parents who are crazy about each other. Through an affectionate, mutual, committed union, bound by sex, you give your kids security, happiness, and a model for marriage that statistics say they'll likely imitate.

Put this relationship first, only behind time with your Father.

> Love is as strong as death,
>   its jealousy unyielding as the grave.
> It burns like blazing fire,
>   like a mighty flame.
> Many waters cannot quench love;
>   rivers cannot wash it away.
> If one were to give
>   all the wealth of his house for love,
>   it would be utterly scorned. (Song of Songs 8:6-7)

Amen and amen.

WEEK FOUR

Mom

(Naomi)

Meet Pleasure

I recently became aware of a grievance I've committed. I'll call it "Picture Day Trauma: A Mother's Obsession." Apparently, standing my kids in front of the mirror coaching them how to smile normally rather than like a serial killer has left an emotional scar. "Don't let them brush your hair with that wet comb. Don't eat ketchup. Smile regular, for Pete's sake! What is that face you're making?" My kindergarten daughter literally handed her pictures over dejectedly and said, "I'm sorry."

This complaint has been confirmed by the men in my life. My husband said the fake-smile pressure his mom applied was so intense that he bears residual anxiety to this day. My Friend Mark hid his fourth-grade pictures for three months because he neglected three of the five "picture-moment rules" his mother established. When I asked my Friend Andrew, he went dark and said quietly, "I don't want to talk about it."

Motherhood. Lord knows we try, but messing up our kids seems inevitable. My girlfriends and I pray we'll be bit parts rather than the lead characters in our kids' therapy sessions. There's hardly anything we knew about less when we first got started, but nothing we want to do better.

If you're not a mom, please don't bail out this week. There's still a lot you can get out of Naomi's story. You can project ahead or consider your history with your mother. Feel free to skip the questions you're positive will never, ever apply to you. (But don't be too sure: You never know when children—stepchildren, adoptive children, your sister's children—may happen to you.)

Before we get into it, what expectations of motherhood fuel your Mom Guilt? Being a room mom? Traditional domestication? Kids who never make bad choices? Producing prodigies? What else?

Let's look at a mom who got some of it right and some of it wrong (just like us): Naomi. We meet Naomi around the same time as Hannah. Israel, not exactly a nation but more a loose association of tribes bound by the same deliverance, was ruled by judges. The Israelites had been in the Promised Land almost three hundred years. The time frame was about 1100 BC, nearly one hundred years before David took the throne.

Read Ruth 1:1 and Genesis 19:30-37. The nation of Israel was birthed through the faith of Abraham. How would you guess the nation of Moab progressed from this drunken, incestuous beginning?

The Moabites were bitter enemies of Israel. The Hebrew prophets denounced idolatrous Moab for bewitching Israel from the time they entered the Promised Land and inhabited land that once belonged to Moab. The law stated that no Moabite—or his sons to the tenth generation—could enter the assembly of the Lord. The Mesha Stele, also called the Moabite Stone (a large inscribed stone attributed to King Mesha of Moab), boasts of Moabites massacring entire Israelite towns.[1] The two nations were separated by only eight miles of

the Dead Sea—Israel on its west, Moab on its east. God said, "Moab is my washbasin," a place barely suitable to wash his dusty feet off (Psalm 60:8). The Old Testament is loaded with their bloody confrontations.

 Read Ruth 1:2. What thoughts must have gone through these parents' minds to take their family to Moab?

What emotions did Naomi likely suffer through?

Elimelech means "my God is King," an apt name for those times. God preferred Himself as the King of Israel, meeting their needs and protecting their faith. He appointed judges to keep order, but He was the sovereign leader. Sin or selfishness wouldn't spoil the throne; no chance of a misdirected authority. *My God is King* would submit to God's dominion, convenient or not, allowing a famine to reform a heart rather than running to a godless enemy.

Naomi means "pleasure," rooted in the fall of man. It beckons us away from a sovereign God who might not attend to our pleasures like we want. It chooses "me" over obedience, over patience. It's the world's siren song, seducing us away from God's discipline, His shaping of our souls. *Pleasure* would choose the banquet table of idolaters over the redemptive work of discomfort.

When *My God is King* married *Pleasure*, bitterness was inevitable. The stage was set for a parenting disaster. That union produced Mahlon and Kilion, which mean "sick" and "pining away."[2] These children were disadvantaged from the day of their birth. Because their parents chose relief over their sons' spiritual integrity, the young boys were on unholy ground, consorting with the enemy. Elimelech and Naomi removed their children from their faith, their tabernacle, their family, and their King to escape a famine the other Hebrews survived just fine.

*Did one or both of your parents choose *pleasure* over *my God is King?* Did you grow up in a Moab? How did it affect you?

Were they running from their own personal famine? What was it?

*Believer, which have you chosen? Are you raising your kids on God's holy ground or in enemy territory, removed from His authority? There is no neutral ground.

No one sets out to ruin her children. It's just that chasing pleasure seems more agreeable than serving a King, especially when famine strikes on His watch. It's one thing when you're on your own, but if you're a mother, children get dragged into your misery. They don't have the resources or maturity to decide otherwise. Kids can't separate themselves from their parents' choices. They have that chance later, but the work is intense, and many never break the cycle.

Are you parenting your kids based on pleasure? Expectations? Keeping up? Fear? What motives drive your parenting?

*What choices are those motives causing you to make? Think critically.

Friend, it is far superior to live in famine under God's hand than in abundance away from His favor. That abundance calls us though, I know. "Come live here; you'll love it. It's way better than that sacrificing you're doing over there. Our gods don't require much from you. Look how happy we are! Your kids? Oh, they'll be fine. Kids are resilient; it'll all work out."

It's an ancient lie as effective today as it was then.

Read Ruth 1:3-5. How did Elimelech and Naomi's choices affect their sons?

Sweet Friend, if your own godliness has taken a backseat to expectations or pressure, how are your choices influencing your children now?

Staying the course they're on, what could you expect from your kids in five years? Ten years?

Naomi's sons spent ten years removed from the tabernacle and married foreign women who worshiped idols. What else would they have chosen? Moab was the only environment they knew, selected by their parents. And born disadvantaged physically and spiritually, no sooner were they married than they were buried. All that was left in the "safe haven" of Moab were three childless widows without a penny to share. It seems like a story of ruin.

But this is a story of redemption.

If your own famine has endangered your children, or if you suffer from being raised in a Moab, there is hope for you, Dear Friend. Our God rescues us from the brink of death. He can heal you from a devastating childhood, and He can redeem the mistakes you've already made with your children.

Naomi blew her first pass at parenting. *My God is King* was forsaken for *pleasure*, which turned to *bitterness* (Ruth 1:20). But our God is merciful. He gave Naomi a second chance at motherhood. He forgave her mistakes and entrusted her with a new daughter to love and lead. A daughter so precious, so dear, so special that she was chosen for the lineage of God's own Son. See, our God is not a punisher.

He's a Redeemer.

Believer, will you face your history with God? Will you let Him separate you from your parents' mistakes? Ask Him to identify the dwelling place you've chosen for your children and pray for the strength to live on holy ground.

Friend, if your childhood was so painful that it has damaged your soul, please seek Christian counseling. Sometimes growing up in a Moab is more than we can walk away from on our own. For your sake, for your children's sake, get professional help to heal those wounds.

Cutting the Apron Strings

My sweet neighbor Heather and I had a laugh the other day. She goes to a Mormon church located half a mile from ours. Both church buildings are new and on the same side of the street. She told me how a twentysomething girl visited their church one Sunday. She came in, looked around a bit, and then took a seat finally. Heather quickly figured out that she had meant to visit my church — a band, lots of other twenty-somethings, nondenominational — but she landed herself in an LDS service.

About the time the Book of Mormon cracked open, her neck started getting blotchy. Heather's anxiety was at alarming levels for this girl because her face said, "The website said there was a band!" I told Heather she probably scooted out of there before they sent her on a two-year mission to Omaha or revoked her caffeine privileges.

You know that moment when you figure out you're in the wrong place?

Naomi did.

God wasn't mean. It really is that bad apart from God's fellowship. He allowed the inevitable. The abundance of Moab

is a lie. It's a bait and switch that has taken many casualties. At the first sign of famine, the Enemy seduces us away from God's protection and then enjoys a front-row seat for our devastation when Moab turns out to be worse.

 Have you ever felt spiritually lost as a mom? What had to happen for you to see?

Read Ruth 1:6-13. Why did Naomi urge the girls to stay in Moab?

Notice the difference between this Naomi and the one in verse 1. Verse 1 Naomi had no problem dragging her sons to an idolatrous foreign land. There is no mention of her hesitation, no attempt to preserve their faith. Elimelech and Naomi were more concerned with their sons' short-term relief than their long-term future. They tethered them to their choice, and it became permanent. Her sons never experienced adulthood.

But she figured out that she had taken them to the wrong place. It was time to go home. And this time, she cut her daughters-in-law loose. Rather than cling to them for her future, as she was too old to marry, she put their best interests above her own. She wanted them safe, with their families, eventually married to other men who would care for them. She wouldn't take them to a land where they'd be despised.

It was time to let go.

If tethering your children to your side and perpetuating their dependence is a 1, and mothering them toward independence by cutting the apron strings is a 10, where do you fall? Why do you say that?

It's a confusing journey God puts moms on. We can barely be apart from our babies for twenty minutes at first. Eighteen years later, we're supposed to send them into the world

responsible, independent. The timeline between those two extremes is about eight hundred bottles of Advil, fifty books on parenting, and eight seasons of Dr. Phil DVDs.

Putting our kids' best interests first means accepting this fact: They'll live most of their lives outside our homes. We either equip them for success or stunt their growth, sometimes irreparably. Keeping your kids glued to your side cripples their ability to become independent.

Here's the trick: Those muscles of responsibility must be exercised all along; otherwise, they atrophy and our kids can't stand on their own two feet when it's time. When we do everything for them, they never learn to do anything on their own. The real tragedy is that they don't even know they can. Our goal is not to raise boys and girls but to produce men and women.

*Why do mothers have a hard time letting go?

What are your long-term goals for your children? Make sure they are your goals and not what everyone else says they should be.

Look back over Naomi's exchange with the girls. Letting go is hard on both sides. What was the knee-jerk reaction of the girls? Why?

"We don't want to go. We'll stay with you." This is the bent of the immature heart. In my house, it sounds like this: "I can't do that. I'm too little. Will you do it? I don't know how. I don't like growing up. I wish I was a baby again."

Now, my kids are young. Maybe yours say, "I don't feel like doing that. I'm not a slave. This house sucks. I'm never making my kids do all this! My friends' parents pay for everything." Or, "Can I move back in?"

Kids push back when we push them toward independence. Most don't go willingly. Why would they? Your kids aren't idiots. If you're doing their laundry, cleaning up their messes, paying for their mistakes, and funding their parties, they won't say, "You know, Mother, I'd like to take on more responsibility and get a job. And stop cleaning my room, for gracious sakes!"

 *How do your kids respond when you push them toward independence?

How do you respond to their reactions?

This should look different depending on where your kids are on the timeline. Your two-year-old cannot make her own dinner, but if you're doing laundry for a sixteen-year-old, it's time for a Come to Jesus Meeting. In our house, we live by two rules:

1. *What can and should you be doing on your own?* The other day, my three kids (ages four, six, and eight) brought their dirty clothes downstairs to the laundry room, turned them right side out, and separated them into colored piles. Their heads barely reach the top of the washing machine. My husband said, "It's like our own little sweatshop." Your kids can do more than you—or they—think.

2. *Everyone is in charge of his or her own stuff.* This includes everything. Their shoes, backpacks, dirty clothes, clutter, bedroom, bathroom stuff, papers, towels, dirty dishes, trash, clean clothes . . . are not Mama's problem. My sweet husband is not exempt from this. I was losing untold hours picking up things that didn't belong to me. We now have fifteen

minutes of house recovery every night. If it belongs to you, take care of it.

These two rules have changed my life.

When I went to college, I had never done laundry. I didn't know how to clean a toilet. I couldn't manage money. I learned everything by screwing it up as an adult. I adore my parents, but they did too much for us. Sure, Mom tried occasionally, but we pushed back when she did, and she let us win. So when my poor father-in-law came to our first apartment, I served him canned ham because I was a domestic tragedy. Sorry, Bob.

Who is winning in your house? Check your fatigue level if you're not sure.

If you're doing too much, what expectations are you working so hard to meet? Domestic goddess? Doting mother? Need meeter? Who is in the audience you're performing for?

The equipping process has tangible results, but it's ultimately about emotional independence. Not that you'll see those fruits now. You'll get the grumbling, but every person who deals with your adult child will reap the benefits of your training. Gregoire gave some practical advice: "If you can't stand the grumbling and the theatrics, leave the room. . . . The goal is to get them to do the task, not to control their feelings. You are doing your children a favor."[3]

Are you taking too much responsibility for your children? Are you cushioning the sting of their choices? Making all their decisions? Are *you* paying for *their* mistakes? How?

Are you trying to maintain a certain appearance? Mom whose kids are perfect? Family who makes healthy choices? Why won't you let the chips fall where they may?

Your children will never learn if they don't have to reap what they sow. This is how God parents us. Parenting our children toward independence serves them best, and we'll find immense relief as moms. When you stop doing what your children should be doing for themselves—making decisions, cleaning up after them, paying for their choices—you'll be a new woman. You can't live your kids' lives for them. You will all suffer if you try. They are whole, real people created by God to be whole, real adults, and you need to let them get there.

*What do you need to let go of that belongs to them, not you? List everything. Forget what anyone will think about it.

Friend, the Enemy will whisper doubt in your ear: "She can't do that. She needs you. You're abandoning her if you won't step in. It's just easier if you do it yourself. He'll be angry. You'll ruin your relationship. If you don't do it yourself, things will fall apart, and what will people think?" Believer, those are lies he uses to keep your children mired in helplessness while you work to exhaustion—physically, emotionally, spiritually. If he can ruin you both, he can raise up a banner of victory over your home.

Let's learn from Naomi. She chose the healthy adulthood of her daughters-in-law over the easier choice. Though it was painful for both sides, she released her grip and said, "Go. You'll never prosper if I don't let you leave." Look at your children and see future husbands, next-generation mothers. Give them what they need to succeed: responsibility, initiative, and independence. Your future son- or daughter-in-law will thank you.

And those whiny kids who aren't your slaves? They'll thank you, too.

Pray for truth here. Affection for our kids sometimes trumps their best interests. Ask God to show you where the boundaries are not working and where they need to be drawn instead.

Meet Strength

I've taught my kids many things. For instance, when Caleb was two, I was forced to teach him that when he's at church helping the song leader, it's not okay to turn around and drop his pants, shooting the moon at thirty innocent toddlers. That's frowned upon, actually. I also taught my son Gavin that when we're eating outside at Rudy's Barbeque, it's better to make the short trip inside to the bathroom rather than pee in their outside fountain. It makes for bad business. I offered to teach my daughter, Sydney, to read, but she preferred to learn how to do cartwheels. You can lead a horse to water, but you can't make her drink if she'd rather do gymnastics.

These issues mattered at the time. But when I'm interceding for my children, I don't labor over these details. Rather, I beg the Holy Spirit to draw my kids early and urgently to His side because nothing I teach them matters if they don't love their Redeemer. My highest calling as a mom is to point my kids to Christ.

Naomi did this terribly at first, but she came around. Let's learn from her progression.

Read Ruth 1:14-18. What qualities do you see in this new daughter entrusted to Naomi's care?

List each of your children and the top three qualities each exhibits.

Ruth committed herself to Naomi's God after worshiping Chemosh, the Moabite national deity. In fact, inscribed on the Mesha Stele, now housed in the Louvre, King Mesha of Moab declared, "I took the vessels of Yahweh, and I presented them before the face of Chemosh."[4] See, the Moabites came from the same ethnic stock as the Israelites, having descended from Abraham's nephew. They were aware of Israel's God, Yahweh, but rejected Him for an idol.

So for Ruth to choose Yahweh over Chemosh was no small concession, but she had a partial knowledge of Him at best. The burden fell to Naomi to show Ruth why Yahweh was superior to any other god. Ruth listened to everything Naomi said about God, exactly as our kids do with us. Their immature beliefs are shaped by our influence, just as Ruth's were by Naomi's.

 Read Ruth 1:19-22. What do you think went through Ruth's mind when she heard Naomi say this? Put yourself in her shoes.

Our children are spiritually fragile. Their faith is immature, mostly untested. Until the end of adolescence, their beliefs are largely a reflection of ours. They are watching, listening, trying to find out if this whole thing is a waste of time. Is this real? Kids can spot a fake in half a second.

So if all they hear from their mom is, "Call me Mara, because the Almighty has made my life very bitter," their perception of faith will be darkly tainted. If God, and by extension His church, is the whipping boy of your distress and that's what

your children hear and see, why would they want anything to do with Him? If a relationship with God seems to produce only bitterness in their mother's life, they'll run in the opposite direction of a faith that seems so defective.

*When your kids add together you and God, what do they get?

I know sometimes we really are empty. I'm not denying your pain, nor do I think you should. It's just that kids equate God with their parents. We're the ones bringing them to church; we're the ones saying it's important. So when our attitudes belie that truth, our kids transfer that to God: He doesn't provide. He doesn't care. He doesn't show up. I know because my mom's life is bitter.

We will go through low points with God. Fact o' life. But we must shield our children from any anger toward Him because *they cannot handle it*. They can't separate that moment from the other wonderful moments you've had with God. They don't see the big picture of your faith.

God can absorb your spiritual frustrations. So can your husband and your real friends in Christ. You don't burden your thirteen-year-old with your marital problems because it would taint her feelings toward her dad and threaten her security. You must spare her the same unfair influence against her heavenly Father.

How have you influenced your kids toward or away from God? What, if anything, needs to change?

It got better for Naomi. Read Ruth 2:1-3. Ruth "found herself" in the fields of an extraordinary relative. Has God ever intervened in your child's life in spite of you? What did He do for your child?

Two things matter here. First, when a man died and left a childless widow, it was customary for his nearest relative (usually a brother) to marry the widow and produce children in his brother's name. In doing so, the brother protected the widow and guaranteed continuance of the family line. Although Ruth was a Moabite, she was entitled to this second marriage because she married a Hebrew, and his family custom took precedence.

Second, the law instructed landowners to leave the grain the harvesters missed so the poor, the alien, the widow, and the fatherless could pick up the leftovers. Ruth was all those things: a poor, fatherless, widowed alien from Moab. But God had His eye on her. No one is irrelevant in God's economy. He brought her back to the family of *My God is King* and placed her in the fields of Boaz, meaning "strength."

Girls, we can run away. We can leave God's family because we're not getting fed. We can even find ourselves in the company of the Enemy, raising our children without a King. But God would have us full, not empty, and He'll stop the earth from spinning to call us back until we "find ourselves" in the middle of a harvest again, exchanging our weakness for strength.

Read Ruth 2:4-23 (this is a great story). What is different about Naomi in verses 19-22? What do you see?

This is God mending the brokenhearted. He tells us constantly He's good for it. God guided Ruth to Boaz's fields. Boaz "happened" to spot a poor beggar gleaning grain. "By coincidence," the foreman noticed Ruth's work ethic. He'd "somehow" found out who she was and how she'd stuck to Naomi against her own best interests, and he "randomly" mentioned all this to Boaz. So "by luck" Ruth returned to Naomi with a full stomach and enough grain for ten days. This was the *first day* back in God's care.

Oh, Girls, this is how the Lord God of Israel's wings provide refuge. He cares for our children beyond our best efforts and in spite of our worst mistakes. The safest place in the universe for our kids is under those wings. As moms, we will disappoint our children. There will be times our selfishness eclipses their needs.

But their God will never let them down.

He can go with our kids to those places we wish we could go but can't: to circumstances outside our watchful eyes, to every fearful encounter our kids face, even to the depths of their souls, often out of reach for a mom. God can go there. The Holy Spirit hedges our kids in better than we can. He sees their future, so He knows how to protect them.

*How does this address the many concerns you have for your kids (college, making the cheerleading team, dating, Myspace.com . . .)?

Have you become distracted with worries and neglected to put your kids under God's wings? Why? Do you trust your own efforts for them more than God's?

What good is it when my son gets into Harvard if he doesn't care about God's will for his life? How have I contributed to my daughter's decision-making skills if I never nurtured her relationship with the Holy Spirit, the ultimate Guide? There are plenty of successful, financially stable adults with gaping holes in their souls. Girls, there is nothing better we can give our children than a foundation for a God-centered life. No one can care for them better than He will.

Now, Boaz was a kinsman-redeemer in Naomi's family. He was responsible for protecting needy family members—redeeming lost land, relatives sold into slavery, widows left behind, or honor if it had been stolen. *Redemption* means

"the purchase back of something that has been lost, by the payment of a ransom."[5] Not by canceling a debt or bargaining a trade, but by paying the price to restore someone who couldn't afford the cost of freedom.

How is Jesus our Kinsman-Redeemer?

What can we learn from Naomi in Ruth 2:22?

When we point our kids to their Redeemer, we give them hope, security, even eternity. Our window of influence is small; ask any empty nester. No sooner are they hanging on our every word than they're walking down the aisle. Busyness and self absorption keep us from deliberately training our kids in godliness. "They'll get it from church," we say. "It's part of our family; they'll see that."

What they'll see is that we dragged them to church but never talked to them about what real faith looks like. We didn't crack open our Bible and point them to God's wisdom. We never held their sweet hands and prayed about their problems. We didn't ask them spiritual questions, what they were learning, what they were struggling with. We never talked about what God was doing in our lives. We failed to enforce godly friendships and let them run with Moabites instead. We didn't teach them the relevance of their Redeemer, so they never saw it.

*Besides taking them to church, how do you tangibly point your kids to Jesus? If you don't, can you say why?

For you, what parenting issues tend to overshadow this one?

My Girlfriends in Christ, let's rise up as mothers and reclaim our children for the namesake of their Father. There is an intersection between their Lord and every concern we face

with them. These are not compartmentalized parenting issues. God belongs in every cheerleading tryout, each final exam, every painful relationship our kids encounter. Let's raise them deliberately in the family of *my God is King*, have them work in fields of *strength*. Even if they drift, that foundation will hold. Scripture promises us:

> Train a child in the way he should go,
> and when he is old he will not turn from it.
> (Proverbs 22:6)

Our husbands are vital spiritual leaders, but it's often in the tenderness of a mother that children learn about the wings God spreads over them. You don't have to be perfect, but when you walk spiritual steps with your kids and your relationship with Jesus reflects your words, you send them into the fields of their Redeemer. There they will be safe, provided for, adored, and ultimately united with the Lord of the Harvest.

What do you need in order to point your kids to Christ? Information? There are a million books on Christian parenting. Support? Ask a godly friend to encourage you. Courage? Pray for it. There is nothing God wants more for your children.

Mom Knows Best

I'm in that stage of parenting when I often check the mirror to see if blood is trickling out of my ears. There isn't a moment when one of my kids isn't talking to me. I've called my husband and begged him to stay on the phone with one of them for five minutes so I wouldn't be forced to puncture my ear drums with a fork.

Once I was driving to Kansas by myself with all three kids, and they talked over each other for two hundred miles. Their voices got louder, not one second passed without sound, and I snapped. I pulled over on the shoulder of I-35, turned the car off, got out, locked the doors, and started walking in the meadow by the highway. I sat in the grass staring at their three faces pressed against the window and mouthing "Mom," and I cried for ten minutes.

My girlfriends love that story because it makes them feel better about themselves. Some of you are there, too. And others would cut off a limb to get some conversation out of your kids. After eleven years in student ministry, I'm convinced that the largest factor in raising healthy kids is communication. The common denominator in strong

families with great kids is a commitment to talk.

*What was communication like between you and your parents? Gloves off? Guarded? Nonexistent? Fake? Real?

Of the eighty-five verses in Ruth, fifty-nine of them are dialogue. Girls, in our busy worlds full of soccer, gymnastics, book clubs, Bible studies, friends, responsibilities, and activities, we must rediscover the treasure of talking with our kids. They need to know it is safe for them to say anything, ask anything, and discuss anything with us. And the responsibility of making the first move falls to us.

Read Ruth 3:1-6. What emotions do you think drove Naomi to initiate this conversation?

What issue is on your child's plate right now that has you thinking, *We've got to talk about that*? What do you want for your child regarding this need?

Ruth needed a man. She was young and beautiful (I'm projecting here) and certainly of marrying age, yet she was stuck gleaning grain like a pauper. But we don't see Ruth asking Naomi for advice. She didn't discuss her needs, her many questions about men in Bethlehem. No doubt she was concerned about her predicament. But it was Naomi who broached the subject. She took the initiative to counsel this sweet daughter toward hooking a man.

If you've spent three seconds around a teen, you know this is still true. Our kids have so many questions; we'd freak out if we knew half of them. They want to know about truth, sex, their bodies, the other gender, drinking, being believers, dealing with their peers, dealing with life. They need your help, but they probably won't ask you.

*How is communication between you and your kids? Is it open? Pretty shut up? Somewhere in between? Describe it.

Do you initiate real conversation with your kids? If so, how's that going? If not, what holds you back?

What are your goals for your relationship with your kids, both short-term and long-term?

Naomi's counsel probably sounded as crazy to Ruth as it does to us. If this was dating in 1100 BC, let's say yay for progress. But here's what matters: Naomi and Ruth's relationship warranted this level of trust. Their affection was clear, and they'd talked about everything else up to that point. So when Naomi told Ruth to hunker down on Boaz's feet, she did it.

How we talk to our kids when they're sixteen hinges on how we've talked to them all along. By the same turn, our influence is related to the communication we've fostered. If we never say two words about sex but then expect them to heed our advice on boys, it'll be a stretch. But if we've discussed their issues all along, we become their natural choice for those topics we most want to weigh in on. This may get laborious when they're seven and we hear a forty-five-minute dissertation on Pokémon, but it pays off when they're older and feel safe enough to ask how far is too far.

The trick to fostering this relationship with your kids is time. There is no way around it. We need to make hard choices with schedules, both ours and our kids. Think on a daily level first. Maybe you prioritize dinner together. Perhaps you make an after-school ritual of snacks and debriefing. Maybe you lie down with your kids in bed at night. If you and your child enjoy mornings, you could do coffee and hot chocolate before

the normal people wake up. Be deliberate with your car time (translation: your whole life).

The Enemy distracts us with activities and convinces us that they equal time. But no kid fondly remembers his mom for things she signed him up for. In fact, if those replace real time together, they'll produce resentment. Between our kids' teams, clubs, groups, and lessons, we don't have time left to know them. I don't remember half the places my dad took me, but I'll never forget how he lay in bed with my sisters and me every night to talk.

Are you too busy? Are your kids too busy? If so, where should you free up your schedules? Think critically, Friend. A healthy relationship with our kids frequently requires sacrifices.

*Where can you work in daily undivided time for your kids?

In doing so, you establish a given: "I care about you, your life matters to me, and I'm here for you." I recommend you listen more than you talk. Kids want to be heard, not lectured. A recent survey asked teens, "If you don't talk to your parents, why?" The highest response was, "Because my parents don't listen to me." Josh Weidmann wrote, "When teens ask you to listen, what they really want is for you to get involved in their lives. Listening may begin as shooting the breeze, but chances are, it'll go deeper soon. For teens to ask you to listen to them is really a plea for heart-interaction."[6]

This creates a culture of communication in your home. Discussions won't be limited to the moments we've scheduled. Once your kids feel safe, they'll likely talk to you at the table, at the store, in the kitchen, after their games—whenever they need to.

I realize some of you are drowning today. The idea of creating time for your kids is like saying, "Come up with a million dollars." I'll ask you this again: What are your goals for your relationship with your kids? If you listed anything beyond meeting their basic physical needs, you'll have to make real time for them.

I said it earlier, but it bears repeating: You cannot have it all, no matter how our culture brags otherwise. We're told to chase the high-powered career, spectacular family with over-achieving kids, passionate marriage, and clean house to boot.

That life does not exist.

Are you chasing that life? If so, where do you feel most deficient?

I began working from home this school year, and it became clear that I truly couldn't do it all. I made the hard choice to pull out of classroom work at my kids' school. I could give them time either during the school day or when they got off the bus at three o'clock. Work had to go somewhere, and the two free mornings I had each week belonged to my three-year-old.

You cannot keep adding. Balance means making hard choices, regardless of what anyone else thinks. Sweet Friend, you can't have it all. And no one role can take all of you without sacrificing the others. It is possible to pursue balance, but when you're chasing the lie, something will give.

*Think about your life right now. What will you look back on in fifty years and say, "I wish I hadn't spent so much time on that"?

Time is a constant; you'll get no more tomorrow than you have today. You'll not get one day back, either. You'll get the same 168 hours a week until the day you die. Time cannot be saved; it can only be spent. You must determine *your* goals and

structure your life around them. Give your time to those goals as best you can, release what you can't, and *let go of the guilt.*

Read Ruth 3:7-18. Ruth's action was a request for marriage to her kinsman-redeemer according to Jewish law, and it worked. Is there an area in your child's life where you need to lay her at Jesus' feet and let Him redeem her? Have you pointed her to that place?

Naomi commissioned Ruth to the care of Boaz, and she returned full. He did not take advantage of her but blessed her as a father, encouraged her as a friend, promised her as a kinsman-redeemer, rewarded her as a patron, and sent her away with gifts and hope. Ruth left Naomi a poor widow and returned a beloved bride.

What can our Redeemer do for your children? Do they know how to get to Him? Have you taught them their position in Jesus? Have you told them how He spreads His garments over them? Do they understand their right to ask for redemption? Have you made them aware of Jesus' stunning goodness? Ruth knew because of the loving counsel of the only mother she had.

Girls, don't wait for your kids to come to you. Make yourself available. Tell them there's nothing they can't talk to you about. Listen with all the interest you can summon. Don't patronize their dramatic feelings or invalidate their emotions. Major on the majors and let the minors go. Who cares what their hair looks like? Do I need to remind you how we teased our bangs? Be honest. Talk about sex and friends and school. Don't criticize. Remember that puppy love feels real to the puppy. Be a listener. Be available.

One day you'll say, "I know a Guy. Here's how you get to Him. . . ."

And they'll listen.

Do you need to release inhibitions about honest conversation with your kids? Ask the Spirit to show you barriers and pray for strength to pull them down.

Refresh

*W*e can't study Ruth and not finish it. There's hardly a more beautiful portrayal of grace. This story mimics our relationship with Jesus, and it's nearly caused me an aneurism not to go there.

Spend a few minutes asking the Holy Spirit to meet you in the Word today. Pray each verse will intersect your life where He wants it to. Ask for a soft heart and keen ears.

So Ruth basically asked Boaz to marry her, and he enthusiastically agreed. One problem: There was a kinsman-redeemer in the family closer to Naomi than Boaz was, and Jewish protocol gave him the right to redeem Naomi's land—and her daughter-in-law—first. If he refused, the responsibility would fall to Boaz.

Read Ruth 4:1-4.

- That very day Boaz called a town meeting on the matter. What does this teach us about affection for our partner? What do you see?
- What does his urgency teach us about mutuality in marriage? Boaz was a wealthy landowner, and Ruth was a poor Moabite widow.

- You know Ruth and Naomi were listening in the bushes. How do you think Ruth felt when the other kinsman-redeemer accepted the responsibility?

Read Ruth 4:5-12.

- Marrying Ruth was not acceptable to the other man, so Boaz stepped in. What substitute kinsman-redeemers have failed to deliver your kids?
- The elders spoke prophetically. Why did they reference Rachel and Leah? How were these women significant to the house of Israel? Check out Genesis 35:22-26, 49:28.

Read Ruth 4:13-22.

- Naomi's hard work paid off. Where have you seen the fruits of your work in the lives of your kids? A good choice? Restoration? A relationship? If you're still waiting, where are you hoping to see it?
- How has God sustained you as a mother? Do you need Him to step in today? Ask. He has given you that right.
- Naomi's sons died without children, but through Ruth, she was given a second chance. It's never too late, Friend. Do you need a second chance as a mother? God can redeem your kids no matter where they are.
- Ruth means "beauty." What was beautiful about Ruth?

Oh, Girls, this is such a story of redemption. God took two penniless widows from the pits of Moab to abundance. Believer,

when *my God is King* settled for *pleasure*, they produced *sick* and *pining away*, and the house was full of sadness. This is what happens when we raise our children apart from God's security. Rejecting His authority in our homes in favor of our own comforts will render us and our children empty.

But it's never too late, no matter how bad it's gotten.

Boaz and Ruth had a son named Obed, meaning "worship."

There our story is complete.

When the *strength* of the redeemer married the *beauty* of humility, the house was full of *worship*. This is second-chance parenting at its best. We serve a God who obnoxiously redeems our parenting mistakes. He is looking for the house that prefers His lordship over pleasure. This originates with parents, but it is realized in the children. When famine comes, that home is safe, and those kids learn true worship.

Obed had a son named Jesse. Jesse's youngest baby, the least likely of his household, was named David. And plucked from the shepherd's fields, he was placed on the throne. God saw fit to use a Moabite, the result of second-chance parenting, in the lineage of His greatest king.

And ultimately, this same family line produced Joseph, who had a son named Jesus. And one day, every knee will bow and every tongue will confess that He is the King of kings (Romans 14:11). "He will be great and will be called the Son of the Most High. The Lord God will give him the throne of his father David" (Luke 1:32). And the house will be full of worship.

> Honor and great power are with Him. *Strength* and *beauty* are in His holy place. Give to the Lord, O families of the nations, give to the Lord the honor and strength that He should have. (Psalm 96:6-7, NLV)

Professional and Daughter

(DEBORAH)

Working Girls

My Girlfriend Trina's daughter, Hannah, was talking about her future. Now, Hannah is a skilled button pusher when it comes to her mom. So understanding Trina's active professional life and how deeply she values education and career, Hannah knew just what to say when Trina asked her about college:

"I'm not going to college. I'll just get married and have babies."

Even knowing that Hannah was manipulating her into a little monkey dance of overreaction, Trina still succumbed: "What?! That is ridiculous! You are no more going to get married without going to college than I'm going to church without a bra on! You can forget that! And if you engineer a wedding when you're eighteen years old, then you'll know just where to find me. I'll be the drunk mother-of-the-bride passed out on the dance floor! Just step over me and dance your way into a life of disappointment and regret!"

Hannah couldn't have been more pleased with her reaction, even if I've embellished it just a tad.

Now, Hannah is nine, so I'm not sure we have a bona fide crisis on our hands just yet, but we dream about our children's

futures like we dreamed of our own. God created us for work. Solomon told us,

> Appetite is an incentive to work;
> hunger makes you work all the harder.
> (Proverbs 16:26, MSG)

Who created that appetite within us? God gives us a hunger for our passion, a physical need to discover our work.

 *What hunger did God put in your life? What work did He design you to do?

If you're working out of obligation rather than passion, how are you feeling?

Now, work should be distinguished from a job. Work is born out of passion and executed through our unique talents. For some women, work is a full-time deal. God gave them a math mind or a penchant for leadership. He gave them a professional dream that can be realized only in a full-time work setting. Or perhaps the full-time aspect is mandatory; mortgages tend to be inflexible. For others, their passionate work is at home with their family. They'd be miserable any other way. Maybe your work is in the service you do, the cause or need or people group you obsess about. Plenty of life work never earned a paycheck.

Here is what I want to say about this: There is no biblical formula for being a working woman. Nowhere does it say we must be housewives exclusively. Nowhere does it say we must be employed full-time. In fact, there are women in Scripture at both ends and in the middle of the work spectrum. God led them all to their work capacity.

How is your current work situation going for you? Why?

*If you could have it any way you wanted it, what would work look like for you?

If you judge other women who work differently than you do, stop it right now. Concluding that other women's work should look like yours is like saying everyone should favor lasagna because you do. I mean, lasagna is delicious, but some girls just prefer fish. Some girls don't have any choice. We have diverse callings, families, circumstances, and goals that God alone knows how to manage. We're turning on our teammates when we draw these dividing lines. We're all serving the same Coach, and as Paul reminded us, "Who are you to judge someone else's servant? To his own master he stands or falls. *And he will stand, for the Lord is able to make him stand*" (Romans 14:4).

Do you impose your work convictions on others, maybe behind their backs? Why?

*Has someone else made you feel guilty or dumb because of your choices? How have you let that affect you? Are you employed (or not employed) because of other people's opinions?

Do you feel like you have no choice, and you're mad at everyone who does? How do you respond to Romans 14:4, quoted earlier? Do you feel able to stand?

Remember Hannah's and Naomi's context? They lived in the three-hundred-year period between the Exodus from Egypt and the establishment of the monarchy, around

1375–1050 BC. A cyclical pattern emerged among the Hebrews during this time: (1) national rebellion, (2) foreign oppression, (3) cries of distress, and (4) God's deliverance. To lead His people from step 3 to step 4, "The LORD raised up judges, who saved them out of the hands of these raiders. . . . Whenever the LORD raised up a judge for them, he was with the judge and saved them out of the hands of their enemies as long as the judge lived" (Judges 2:16,18).

This was perhaps the darkest period of Israelite history, centered on their refusal to purge their land of all things Canaanite. They abandoned their identity as God's chosen nation and adopted pagan morals, gods, and religious practices. Only by allowing foreign oppressors and then raising up godly leaders (most of them more like military commanders than judges in the modern sense) did God preserve the embryonic kingdom from extinction. During this three-hundred-year period, God commissioned twelve judges: eleven men and one strong woman.

Read Judges 4:1-5. From these verses, list every role and responsibility Deborah had.

In this circumstance, what professional pressures did Deborah likely endure that we still experience today?

Don't you love the casualness of verse 4? "Deborah . . . was leading Israel at that time." Sister had a full-time career, to say the least. What can we learn from her?

One, when it was time to work, she loaded up, fought morning traffic, and sat in her office under the Palm of Deborah. There was a clear distinction between Home Deborah and Work Deborah. God made sure to include that detail in His Word. At the palm, she put on her work face and got down to business. But you better believe no warring Israelite neighbors followed

her home. Work was reserved for the Palm of Deborah.

We do our families a huge service to leave our work at work. Coming home means shaking off the day's disappointments, taking deep breaths to clear our minds. Our kids and husbands become the victims of our professional frustrations because we can't flick our boss on the head for his irrational demands or scream at our coworker's ignorance. So we bottle those feelings up, drive them home, and unleash them on the most innocent bystanders.

You feeling me? Have you done this? What is so hard about making this distinction?

What would be the long-term effects of this behavior on your family?

Now, my Palm of Deborah is my home, but I still have to draw a line between Work Jen and Home Jen. I've scheduled specific time to work, and no matter what kind of groove I'm in, when the kids walk in the door, I have to switch hats. My scales sometimes tip here, but my kids don't care about my Bible studies. They just need me to be Mom. They'll remember which I chose.

*Discuss with your small group some strategies for switching hats when it's time. Write down your thoughts.

Because I juggle many roles and am prone to drama, I'm aware of my spaz-out potential. I cannot express how much I *don't* want to be the wife and mom who falls apart every time she encounters pressure. So when my roles start to squeeze together, I pray something simple: "Lord, please keep the wheels on."

That may not seem profound, but God keeps the wheels

on when they should be flat, blown, or hijacked altogether. I have conferences the next two weekends, I'm volunteering at two "fun field days" next week, and this very study is due in fifteen days. I started praying for the wheels a month ago, and God has kept them on. I'm only mildly stressed, and if you knew me, you'd declare this a miracle on par with the Jesus french fry on eBay.

How do you cope with professional stress? Is it healthy? Is God showing you a better option?

One more thing from verse 5: Among Deborah's other responsibilities, the Israelites came to her to settle disputes. She was a worthy judge. Professionally, it is a nonnegotiable quality to be decisive. Girls, we need to make up our minds. Insecure decisions are a detriment to you and every person under your leadership.

Girl, God put you in the position you're in. He gave you a smart mind and the Holy Spirit, the origin of discernment. Use the common sense the Lord gave you. That eliminates a host of bad choices. Then go to your skills: What do you know, what have you experienced, what does your business savvy tell you, what are you equipped to do? Next use wise counsel. Listen to smart people and weigh their opinions. Finally, seek the Spirit. You'll get a green or red light from Him if you'll listen quietly. Line all those up and go, Girl.

Do you have a professional decision you need to make up your mind on? Or is your professional life marked by indecision? What have you discovered from the process just outlined?

Maybe your indecision has to do with your entire job or the circumstances you're working in. It may be because your hands feel tied; you need to work as much as you do, and

your options are limited. You'd like to work less or differently, but you can't. Or perhaps you're addicted to your paycheck and are unwilling to make lifestyle changes to enable a career change. Maybe your work situation is toxic, and indecision has kept you from pursuing a healthier option.

 What motivates you to work (passion, money, responsibility, status . . .)? Try to be honest.

You wrote earlier what your ideal work situation would look like. What keeps you from pursuing that position or capacity?

Even if your hands are truly tied, the writer of Hebrews reminds us that God "set a certain day, calling it 'Today'" (4:7). If you're unhappy and yet have no options to change your circumstances, remember that God's forte is Today. He comes Today. He encourages Today. He can maximize your Today, regardless of how you feel about it. Will you give Him Today and let Him use it?

And don't let indecision paralyze you in a toxic work situation. Life is too short; you don't want to neglect what really matters to you—family, friends, passionate work. You'll blink, and it'll all be over. Solomon declared, "There is nothing better for a man than to enjoy his work" (Ecclesiastes 3:22). If you're looking at work saying, "Someday . . . ," why not chase after that dream? It's never going to fall into your lap. How many years will you waste?

Follow Deborah's lead. She was so strong that God set her over His whole nation. She made decisions for a living, and you can bet she didn't waffle back and forth. In fact, her decisiveness drew people to her like a magnet, and they followed her leadership because she exuded confidence.

Whether your work is at an office or at home or both, let work time be work time, and when it's time to be a mom

and wife, be a mom and wife. In both places, be certain. Be decisive. Be discerning. God uses His strong girls. He looks down every morning and asks, "Who can I use Today?"

Ask the Spirit to reveal your health in this area. Take your decisions to Him; pray for discernment and confidence.

It Takes a Village To Be a Professional

Let me tell you the best part about being a schoolteacher: room moms. When I started teaching, I'd just emerged from the isolated world of college, where you sink or swim on your own merits. Hard work earned you a degree; hard partying earned you a spot at the junior college next to your mom's house.

So when the moms of my fourth graders began circling at Back-to-School night asking for jobs and responsibilities, I thought I had died and gone to Helper Land. "We'll plan the parties. We'll bring the crafts. We'll do your bulletin boards since you subtly declared you hate them. If you need something else, let us know."

I also discovered that fourth-grade girls could grade multiple-choice tests, and they'd give up a month of recesses to do it. Not far behind was the high school program that sent students to help. My sister Lindsay even graded spelling tests once, but she was removed from her job after making fun of a nine-year-old for misspelling *leotard* as *le-o-pard*, until we told her it was leopard, l-e-e-e-eopard. She said no geniuses can spell (or read, apparently).

What is it about women that compels us to do it all? "No, I don't need help. Thank you, but I can do it." Darn it, we've worked so hard to get where we are. Women have more opportunities than ever; the glass ceiling has shattered. So heck if we're going to ask for help and appear needy. But perhaps we can learn a thing or two from Deborah, leader of Israel.

Read Judges 4:1-5 again. Jot down who's who if that helps keep the players straight. Now read Judges 4:6-7. What good leadership do you see Deborah exercise here? What other options might she have rejected?

This power struggle was in the north and was particularly intense near the tribes of Naphtali, Zebulun, and Issachar. Deborah reigned from land belonging to the tribe of Ephraim, eighty miles south of the afflicted area. It wouldn't have made a lick of sense for her to rally the southern troops, load up all their supplies, and journey eighty miles north through rocky terrain to fight this battle. Using wise leadership, she delegated this role to Barak, a military leader living in the war zone.

Now, I'm no war analyst, but I see a principle of good business. A wise woman takes full responsibility for what belongs to her, and she sets limits on or delegates everything else. Efficient workers understand this balance.

This goes two ways. One, ask who is best equipped to handle a task. Is it yours alone? Do you have an assistant better suited for it? A coworker gifted in this area? Is it too big for one person? Is this a team project? What part, if any, needs to be delegated? Is there anyone who could contribute? A true professional knows when to pass the baton.

*How do you do with delegation? How about asking for help? How have either of these tactics affected your job and the way you feel about it?

I'm a writer. I can't delegate a chapter when I'm tired. No one steps in and meets my deadlines. So my support looks different. My friends discuss content with me; many of their ideas you've already read. My Bible study girlfriends cooked dinners for my family for three straight weeks when conferences, deadlines, and retreats all merged. My husband morphs into Mr. Mom when I need him to. I turn to other writers when I need advice or a sympathetic ear. None of these take work off my plate, but they get under and around my plate, making it easier for me to carry.

If you're a professional island, where else can you find support, advice, encouragement, reprieve? You'll have to ask for this (like I do). Support must be created.

Two, make sure *you* are not getting stuck with someone else's responsibilities. Some people will take advantage of others until the day they die, and they can spot a sucker. They will pawn things off on you for as long as you'll let them. Cloud and Townsend suggest this: "If you are being saddled with another person's responsibilities and feel resentful, you need to . . . realize that your unhappiness is not your co-worker's fault, but your own."[1]

In other words, stop bailing the same person out and covering for his deficiencies all the time. That's your choice. Exceptions are one thing; enabling is another. Let him feel the consequences for his own poor planning or unreliability. Act responsibly toward him by explaining your professional limits and then stick to your guns, Sister.

*Do you set healthy limits professionally? If so, what are they? If not, who are you allowing to take advantage of you? Maybe your boss? Why haven't you set limits?

Any chance you're taking advantage of a hard-working colleague? Do others have to rescue you professionally all the time? Why?

Drawing boundaries at work is challenging because it produces a knee-jerk reaction, especially if someone has made a habit of shirking responsibility or you've taken on too much. This is especially challenging with your boss, but no one will protect your professional health but you. It is possible to discuss this issue with integrity and professionalism. A raging rant won't accomplish much; a rational discussion including possible options can be effective. Confront those who take advantage of you. The short-term awkwardness stings, but the long-term benefits are invaluable—for you and your colleague.

Speaking of knee-jerk reactions, read Judges 4:8-10. Bless him. What does Barak's reaction tell you about Deborah?

Land sakes! Barak was a warrior! A man's man with spears and machismo and such. He was entirely capable of leading this attack. His name means "thunderbolt," for Pete's sake. I'm jumping ahead, but he led a successful assault on their enemies. Barak was so noteworthy that he was included among the heroes of faith in Hebrews 11:32. Yet his first response was to cling to Deborah's robe and whimper, "If you don't go with me, I won't go."

Professionally, what can you learn from this as a Deborah? As a Barak?

I love Barak, frankly. He has given me permission to be terrified and then rise to the challenge. My first reaction is always, "I can't! I'm scared!" Big tasks petrify me, and I immediately feel unworthy, incapable. I usually have a little

argument with God in which I lay out all the reasons He should choose someone else. He listens nicely. He still makes me do it. I beg Him to help me and then leap; God has yet to let me fall.

It's okay to be scared as long as you leap.

And if you're a Deborah, offer the Baraks in your lives two things:

1. Give them the chance to show themselves capable. Barak didn't think he could do it, but Deborah did. She saw his potential and delegated an enormous task to him. Her confidence in his abilities was immeasurable.

2. Give them a break when they falter. Had Deborah despised his insecurity and yanked his opportunity away, no one would have known how capable he truly was. Let those you lead show a little fear sometimes. It doesn't mean they won't still take the bull by the horns.

Be a compassionate leader who empowers your colleagues.

Do you have any unhealthy patterns with either of those work principles? If so, why?

Read Judges 4:12-16. What is the connection between Deborah's role as leader of Israel and her role as prophetess? How did the latter affect the former?

*What are your biggest challenges in merging your spiritual life with your professional life?

Barak needed a mentor. He and Deborah passed the baton back and forth between them. She journeyed to Kedesh to

stand by him, but he summoned the troops. Deborah advised him; Barak carried out the task. She said "go"; he led the army down Mount Tabor. She left the safety of the Palm of Deborah to stand in battle with her protégé. As a card-carrying God follower, she counseled Barak with discernment.

Any savvy businesswoman would herald the benefits of mentorship. There is no substitute for this type of learning. It is the model Jesus used with His disciples. Girls, if you are in the building years of your career and haven't already, seek out a godly mentor. Find a woman in your profession who will invest in you. Watch her, learn from her successes and mistakes, ask questions. Discover how to be a godly woman in a professional setting.

And if you're a seasoned veteran in your career, Wise One, please consider taking on a protégé. Find a young believer in your business and bring her under your wing. Teach her all the things you wish you'd heard at her age. Show her how to merge her godliness with her professionalism. Sometimes we need a Deborah to stand by us in battle until we're confident to lead on our own.

What is your experience with mentorship, if any?

Would you consider finding a mentor or becoming one? Do you have someone in mind? Or if you see obstacles, how can you address them?

I love that Deborah led Israel in the seventh book of the Bible, way too soon to expect to find a girl in that position. God is not boxed in by preconceived ideas on gender. He would empower you professionally, Believer. You are God's own light in your workplace. You are the chalkboard upon which He writes, teaching your coworkers what it means to be godly

professionals: decisive, clear, firm on boundaries, respectable, responsible, empowering, compassionate, and driven by His own Spirit. Oh, the things He can do with you, Friend.

> In the time of Shamgar
>   son of Anath,
> and now again in Jael's time,
> roads were too dangerous
>   for caravans.
> Travelers had to take
>   the back roads,
> and villagers couldn't work
>   in their fields.
> Then Deborah took command,
> protecting Israel as a mother
>   protects her children. (Judges 5:6-7, CEV)

Where would God mold you professionally? Ask the Spirit to show you any areas He would like to work on. Pray to be a Deborah. Every workplace is in need of one.

Live Well

Wouldn't work be such an excellent topic if we didn't also have to discuss being a wife, mother, daughter, friend, neighbor, believer, sister, churchgoer, PTA member, soccer mom, housekeeper, chef, and driver? Oh! And tutor, relationship counselor, ministry volunteer, field-trip sponsor, mediator, bank teller, caregiver, toilet scrubber, baseball team snack coordinator, Bible study contributor, sexual-needs meeter, dishwasher, and crisis counselor?

I'm just saying.

We discussed some professional issues at work: limits, delegation, finding health in the workplace. That's all super while you're there. But frankly, the hardest part is everything else that's supposed to fit in the gaps. From the end of work today to its start tomorrow, we have ten other full-time jobs. For the millionth time, we cannot have it all, Girlfriends. Not because we're not organized multitaskers but because *there isn't enough time.*

On average, how much time each week do you work?

Often work steals our time, and we start pointing fingers: Our boss makes us do it; our coworkers demand it; this project is time-intensive. Usually, the primary person who needs a strong dose of professional limits is staring back from the mirror. Friend, sit down and have a long talk with yourself. Work will grow into the time you give it. And no one will set this boundary for you.

The first step toward this balance is deciding what you can do and when you can do it, while saying no to everything else. Get a handle on how much time and energy you actually have and learn to manage your work accordingly. This means living in reality, not Productive Fantasy Land. Cloud and Townsend suggest that strong communication with others is the key. You might say to someone who is asking more of you than you can do, "If I am going to do A today, I will not be able to do B until Wednesday. Is that okay or do we need to rethink which one I need to be working on?"[2]

Do you tend to take on too much at once? What keeps you from saying no?

Some of your best work is done on unimportant details that don't contribute to your professional goals or responsibilities. Committees, side projects, extraneous meetings, and phone calls can steal entire days. I am *fantastic* at unimportant tasks, yet somehow they don't help me meet my deadlines, and they extend my work time into family time. Individually, these extras don't amount to much time. But string three or four of them together, and I've lost a whole morning.

Does your time get lost on unimportant details? Think critically and list them. They may masquerade as relevant.

*What boundaries could you set to reclaim your time in these areas?

After evaluating task priorities, determine how many hours a week you'll spend on work. You must be Deborah decisive here. If you put limits on office time, you'll be forced to work smarter. When your time is limitless, it's tempting to say yes to everything. If you know you are walking out the door at three o'clock come hell or high water, you'll be less likely to waste time or overcommit.

I work from eight fifteen to twelve fifteen three mornings a week, plus an hour and a half during my son's naptime. That's not much time, so here are my limits: I don't check e-mails, answer my phone, eat lunch, turn on the TV, read new material for research (those books are reserved for the bathtub), do a single domestic task, or waste time on hygiene or vanity.

I've had to work smarter because my time limits are so tight. When I wrote my first book, I would've sworn it could never be done in the time I have now, but my work time was fragmented then. Now my time limits come first—not my deadlines—so I'm forced to fit the latter into the former. And they fit.

It may feel crazy, but can you set time limits with your job? If so, what might your start and stop times be? Maybe you can free up an afternoon? Leave one hour earlier (or on time)? What could you try?

If you don't have this option, could you rearrange your time creatively? For instance, could you come in one hour earlier to leave one hour earlier? Work through lunch to leave earlier? Extend four days a week to shorten Friday? Do you see any possibilities?

Even if you have a willing boss or a flexible schedule, time limits may be freaking you out. Your workload fills up every minute you currently have. I'd ask you to try to make time cuts anyway. Even if it pinches at first, I'm betting you'll learn to work more efficiently and eliminate time stealers from your day, especially if you spend the extra time on your other priorities. Balance is an excellent motivator. Worst case scenario: It doesn't work, and you resume your previous schedule.

Girls, if your workload has taken precedence over every other role, I have to ask: Is this working for you? Are you going to be happy in ten years with the decisions you're making now? In twenty? Please hear me: I'm all about passionate work. My name didn't get on the front of this book by accident. I love what I do. I'm not asking you to abandon your professional passions.

But if work takes 75 percent of your time, there's not much left, is there? Earlier, you identified the reasons you work, and I wonder if any motives lurk that will ultimately leave you unsatisfied. Solomon discovered the following empty pursuits.

Read Ecclesiastes 2:22-25. What was Solomon saying about this anxious striving we do?

This makes sense to me. Think of the largest anxiety on your professional plate right now. What will any of it matter in five years? Yet here it is robbing your peace of mind, keeping you up at night. When work stresses you out to the point of grief, all it's doing is stealing your life away. You'll lose this time—as will your husband, kids, friends—and your losses will matter more than your professional gains.

Girlfriends, as fulfilling as work can be, it will never compare to relationships. God's entire Word declares this. It's not that work isn't necessary or valuable, but when it's at the expense of the most important people in your life, it's a

tragedy. If work cheats others of all your time or all your peace, it will certainly be a regret someday.

*Has work replaced relationships in your life? Which ones?

Read Ecclesiastes 4:4. Why is this motivation like chasing after the wind?

I want you to like me, and I'm about to ruin that. This is so unpopular, I know, but if you're working to keep the house, the cars, the private-school tuition, the right clothes, the right clubs, the status, and the stuff, everyone loses. No, Friend, you don't have to have all that. I don't care who else does. I don't care what their kids have. Working for stuff and status will leave you gasping. You'll also never arrive, by the way—an unfortunate reality of the game.

When our barometer is our neighbor, life simply ceases to be fun. It becomes a constant competition, which our children learn from their front row seats, and no one ever wins. It's an insatiable lifestyle. Solomon wrote,

> Whoever loves money never has money enough;
>   whoever loves wealth is never satisfied with his
>   income. (Ecclesiastes 5:10)

Does keeping up play an unhealthy role in your work choices? Can you pinpoint why you feel the way you do?

*If so, what are you reluctant to sacrifice? Status? Attention? Stuff? Lifestyle? Location? You can be honest.

Without overdramatizing, what would happen if you made that sacrifice?

Listen, I'm not trivializing the need to earn money. Nor am I suggesting that work is always characterized by poor motives or greed. Many of us have to work, many of us love to work, and that's okay. God gives grace for our roles, and it is possible to be effective in each one.

But we don't want to sacrifice motherhood on the altar of office hours, and a promotion is little consolation when our marriage falls apart. The right neighborhood is a sorry substitute for a healthy family. A life that has no time for girlfriends is a lonely life. I know it for a fact.

Let's make sure that our work situation is working for us. Pure motives free us up to make superior choices. We're not dictated by selfishness or pride. Work can be fulfilling, fantastic, and wonderful, but it has the power to crowd out a real life. We don't have to be this person:

> I turned my head and saw yet another wisp of smoke on its way to nothingness: a solitary person, completely alone—no children, no family, no friends—yet working obsessively late into the night, compulsively greedy for more and more, never bothering to ask, "Why am I working like a dog, never having any fun? And who cares?" More smoke. A bad business. (Ecclesiastes 4:7-8, MSG)

Jonathan Swift said, "May you live all the days of your life."[3]

Live well, Friend.

Ask the Spirit to search you today, Believer. Pray for the strength to make the right choices.

Daughter

When I was a teen, my parents were such idiots. They wouldn't spend sixty dollars on a pair of Pepe jeans. Oh no! They were *overpriced*. They didn't let me bring boys to my room. As if I couldn't handle that at sixteen. They were obsessed with knowing who I was with and where we were going. They treated me like a convict. They were always on my back with their curfews and seat belt reminders. It was a miracle I survived given the way they suffocated my freedom.

But I'm so proud of them. They have gotten smarter and smarter since my adolescence. They must have read some books or taken some classes because they're not nearly as impossible as they used to be. They've really matured as parents. As humans. I worried once that they'd never enter the Land of the Enlightened, but today I'm happy to tell you they both live there with me. Took 'em awhile, but they made it.

The journey as a daughter is a tricky one. Our parents go from being our caregivers to being our managers, oppressors, advisors, friends. The dynamic of our relationship with our parents is a moving target, but once a daughter, always a daughter, right? In seeking balance, let's take a brief look at

this role today and see if we can spot any tipped scales.

How would you describe your relationship with your parents today?

How is your answer related to your childhood experience?

Dearest Girlfriends, some of your answers are clouded in abuse, pain, neglect, brokenness. The most fertile soil for dysfunction is a mistreated child. I want to roll that stone away in your life so badly, but I'm not qualified. Envision me on my knees clasping my hands. Please, Friend, seek Christian counseling if you haven't. Don't let those early years rob you of joy today. Every day spent broken in yesterday is another day lost. Go. Let Jesus heal you with the help of an experienced counselor.

Is this you? What did you suffer through as a child? How has it affected you as an adult?

You can't turn back time, but you can decide how you will let your past affect your present. If you were wounded by a parent and have never embraced the healing process, Sweet Girl, you'll stay a wounded mom, a wounded wife, a wounded friend. Your husband, children, and girlfriends can't heal that injury for you. They'll try, but it will never be enough. You'll be angry that they can't love you right, and they'll be devastated because they don't know how. For your sake and that of every person who loves you, choose to deal with it rather than deny it.

This process will guide you to the elusive Holy Grail of forgiveness. Cloud and Townsend wrote, "When you refuse to forgive someone, you still want something from that person, and . . . it *keeps you tied to him forever*. . . . [Forgiveness] ends your suffering, because it ends the wish for repayment that

is never forthcoming and that makes your heart sick because your hope is deferred (Prov. 13:12). . . . Cut it loose, and you will be free."[4]

If you were hurt by a parent and haven't reached forgiveness, what do you still want from that parent? Is this desire keeping you tethered to your pain?

Now, most of us come from a plain old run-of-the-mill averagely dysfunctional family. Our parents did the best they could in raising the compliant, agreeable daughters all of us were. But even though we're all grown-ups now, this relationship still has the potential for messing stuff up. Let's look at two boundary problems a lot of us daughters struggle with.

1. *Failure to launch.* God figured out the winning formula at the beginning: "For this reason a man will leave his father and mother and be united to his wife, and they will become one flesh" (Genesis 2:24). The Hebrew word for *leave* means "to loosen." This seems obvious, but marriage won't work until you loosen bonds from your original family and tie yourself in a double knot around your husband, and he does the same for you. It is no business of your mom's how you spend your money, where you send your kids to school, how your husband ticked you off yesterday, or how you're managing your life. It's only going to be her business if you make it her business.

If you're still trying to earn your parents' approval—and I say this lovingly—get over it. If they don't approve of you yet, it's never gonna happen. Stop catering to your mom's every criticism. Quit bending over backward to accommodate her demands. Stop laying every decision on your dad's chopping block of analysis. If your real allegiance is still to your parents, then your husband and children are getting your leftovers. And don't think they don't know it. There is no winner when you refuse to leave and cleave.

*This is not your mom's problem; it's yours. If you struggle here, what part of the struggle do you own? What boundaries have you failed to set? Be specific.

Why does their approval matter so much to you?

2. *No more sugar daddy.* Another scale that gets tipped has to do with money. This has two extremes. One, your parents keep dishing out the goods, and you feed like a little piggy at the trough. Free vacation? Yes. Down payment on our house? Yes. Buy all our kids' clothes? Yes. Pay for private school? Yes. Fund our activities? Yes. This little purse? Yes. That pair of shoes? Yes.

Stop the insanity! I know we love our goodies, but this is toxic. When we stay on our parents' payroll (or our in-laws' payroll), we forfeit our status as an adult. We sacrifice independence, responsibility, and maturity for the sake of stuff. We teach our kids to live above their means and yank the role of provider away from our husbands. And don't forget the conditions that come with free handouts. This gives parents the "right" to weigh in on your decisions, pass judgment on the way you spend money, and control the way you live.

*Are you feeding at the trough? Why won't you live within your actual means? (And, no, you don't *have* to accept anything. Try this: "No thank you, Mom.")

What are your children learning from your choices?

This scale tips the other way when parents finance their adult child's road of failure and irresponsibility. "I'm in trouble again, Dad. This time it's going to be different." When we rely

on our parents to rescue us from our poor spending habits or foolish decisions, we're guaranteeing a lifetime of failure. Solomon asked,

> Of what use is money in the hand of a fool,
>   since he has no desire to get wisdom?
>   (Proverbs 17:16)

Wisdom learns from financial mistakes and refuses to repeat them. Wisdom discovers the value of saving and living within realistic means. Wisdom pays for her own failures and makes better choices next time. Foolishness chronically overspends, overreaches, refuses to grow up. Parents can throw money at foolishness, but they're just funding the party. They'll have to ante up again soon.

Friend, do your parents or in-laws consistently bail you out financially? What do you have to change to end this destructive cycle? Make a move? Scale down? Get a real job?

Ladies, are you bailing out your grown children? Why won't you let them grow up and feel the sting of their choices? Are you willing?

This is a light treatment of our role as daughters, and I omitted a thousand other things, but the bottom line is this: As an adult daughter, your relationship with your parents should not eclipse your other roles in your home. Your mom should never be the confidante to whom you tear your husband down—nor should anyone else. Your parents should have no information about your finances and the way your family spends money. The way you parent is between you and your hubby. Your mom shouldn't be getting more time with you than your husband or

kids. Your decisions are exactly that: yours.

*If limits need to be set in this relationship, how do you suspect your parents will respond?

What are your goals for this relationship? Communicate those lovingly to your parents.

With those boundaries in place, I'm enjoying my parents now more than ever. I've discovered how funny they are and how things they told me were right after all. We talk about spiritual issues in a mutual way. Defensiveness doesn't ruin those conversations now. We just thoroughly enjoy each other. We'll be vacationing for a couple of weeks in the mountains, and do you know who we voluntarily invited? My parents. Not because we felt obligated, but because we know we'll laugh until someone wets their pants.

They don't know how much money we make, nor do they ask. Mom doesn't lecture me on parenting unless I call for advice. But after living away from them for thirteen years, I've found myself saying, "When are y'all moving to Texas? I want you closer." All their books and parenting classes since I left have really paid off.

An adult relationship with your parents can be wonderful. Where is it getting messed up for you? If it seems irreparable or too late, Jesus can still fix what's broken inside you. Pray for discernment on the very next thing to do to start the process.

Refresh

This day is so important, but many of you will ignore it. Let me just say it: We're talking about rest. I want to intervene before you roll your eyes with a big "as if" or shake your head in anticipation of the guilt you'd feel. Will you pray before we begin and ask God to make you a blank slate in this area? Ask Him to remove any hang-ups you have about making time to care for yourself.

I love the beginning of Genesis because everything was in its purest form: perfect relationship with God, unhindered intimacy between a man and wife, everything pure, the primary elements in place. There is so much to learn from God's first and best ideas.

Read Genesis 1:31–2:3.

- God is immortal, invincible. "He will not grow tired or weary" (Isaiah 40:28). Why on earth did He rest on the seventh day?

- Why do you think God blessed this day above the other six? Read verse 3 carefully.
- Why do you think God saw fit to include such a holy, blessed day of rest at the beginning of His Word, way before temples or priests or commands?

Exactly one month after Israel's deliverance from Egypt and the crossing of the Red Sea, Moses and the Hebrews were making their way to Sinai, where the law would be delivered on the mountain. They'd been traveling through the desert, and their resources had run out. After all, there were a couple million of them. Their stomachs and mouths were growling in unison, so God provided. He sent bread (manna) each morning and quail at twilight. The bread and meat they gathered were good for only that day; they were rotten by the following morning. With one exception.

Read Exodus 16:4-5.

- How was the sixth day different from the others?

Read Exodus 16:21-23.

- This is the first mention of the Sabbath in Scripture; it is from the same root word as *rest*. What tone do you pick up on in God's voice? How does He feel about this?
- The Sabbath had to be planned for. Do you plan for rest? If so, how? If not, why?
- Certainly they could've journeyed on. Work wasn't over. Yet they rested. What can you learn from this first Sabbath? What misconceptions rob you of resting?

Read Exodus 16:24-30.

- God deliberately provided for rest! It was the only day the manna and quail wouldn't spoil from the day before. Do you believe He can provide what you need to rest? What do you need? Ask Him.
- Even if they wanted to collect food on the Sabbath, it wouldn't be there. The Hebrews had to gather it in advance. What does this teach you about your own rest? What do you need to do in advance to get rest?
- How did God feel about the Hebrews who ignored the Sabbath? How would He find you today in this area?

Read Exodus 20:8-11 (part of the Ten Commandments).

- Why do you think God named each person who should rest (son, daughter, servants . . .)? What influence does your rest (or lack of it) have on your family?
- Believer, hear it: The Sabbath is *holy*. Not helpful, not beneficial, not a good idea. It's *holy* to God. How do you feel about rest? What is it to you?
- If God is not too consumed to rest, then you shouldn't be either. How can you set aside time for resting, both for His worship and your recovery?

Anytime I read someone else's work on time management, this is the moment I get irritated. "Oh, sure. I'll just rest. Easy as pie." Believer, I hope you hear today that this is a nonnegotiable. Everyone suffers when you're burned out: you, your family, your work, God, your friends, everyone.

This does *not* mean you must become an inpatient at your local spa or miraculously develop a life of leisure. Rest comes

in many forms: a bath every night, an hour for reading in your favorite chair, working out, an evening walk, time in the Word. Rest is supernaturally delivered through church; that was God's initial design for the Sabbath. Rest is about mental and physical relief. You enjoy it however you want to.

Just remember this: The Sabbath is holy to God. It is not optional, and it's certainly not selfish or lazy. The Sabbath is mentioned 151 times in the Bible.[5] The God of the universe modeled rest at the beginning of time. If it's good enough for Him, it's good enough for you. Please, Friend, decide when and how you will care for your mind and body. I have friends who jog, but that would ruin my day. I want a book and a bath at night. Figure out what your best rest looks like and embrace it guilt-free. Your happiness, your health, and your relationships depend on it.

Bear in mind that the LORD has given you the Sabbath. (Exodus 16:29)

Friend

(MARY, MARTHA, LAZARUS, AND JESUS)

Sweet Beginnings

The boys' basketball coach for the university here goes to our church. He is a dear man and has the sweetest family on the planet. He and his wife are as regular as you and me, and I talk my nonsense around them like anyone else. That said, he's a bit of a local celebrity, having taken the boys deep into the tournament every March. The entire city is grateful. We like our Longhorns to win. This is Texas, after all.

So my Girlfriend Trina tells about the first (and last) time she talked to him. She came face-to-face unprepared and got a little starstruck. Trina panicked, flushed deep red, and—so help me this is true—started reciting her high school basketball stats. You know, because the head basketball coach at a huge Division I school is deeply interested in sophomore girls' basketball in 1983 at Quincy Notre Dame High School (or, as Trina explained to him, "QND"). She wanted to die for days and hasn't made eye contact with him since.

Now, that story is irrelevant except for this: Don't you just love your girlfriends? Aren't they funny? Don't you adore your inside jokes and memories? True friendship is one of my favorite gifts. These moments shared are treasures,

nothing less. Stories like these are our way of laying claim to each other; ultimately we are saying, "I know her. I was there. She's my friend, and I love her."

We're looking at our role as a friend this week. Certainly your husband and kids will get more of you than your friends do. Your job likely demands a huge slice of the pie, too. Having said that, I value my girlfriends like air. I bet you do, too. So did Jesus. He had three special friends, unique from His disciples. And two of them were girls.

Read Luke 10:38-39. This is the first mention of Mary and Martha in Scripture. How do you suppose they got Jesus to come to their house?

This happened in Jesus' final six months or so. The girls lived in Bethany, barely two miles from Jerusalem where Jesus certainly ministered but didn't live. We don't know if they'd met before, but the first time we read of Jesus in Bethany is this instance, the fall before His spring crucifixion. So based on Scripture, Jesus and these siblings had a precious six-month friendship.

I'm sure they'd heard plenty about this young rabbi. He'd caused quite a ruckus on the Mount of Olives, which separated Jerusalem from their small village. Jesus had left behind his popularity and was in His final year of strong opposition. A couple of years ago they could've caught a rising star, but now it was much less fashionable to be a friend of Jesus. He had too many powerful enemies.

They sure didn't care about that.

Maybe they talked to Simon, a leper from their village Jesus had healed. Perhaps they'd sat at the edge of a crowd as Jesus taught. They probably worshiped at the temple while He was there and recognized the Son in His Father's presence. However it went down, word on the street was Jesus

was coming to Bethany, and my bets are on Martha for getting Him into her living room.

Do you have an unlikely friend? What barriers did you step over to engage her?

Martha was probably a widow of considerable means. She had her own home and the resources to host Jesus and all His disciples. So she and Mary were likely quite a few years older than Jesus. Together with their brother, Lazarus, I envision them as quirky sitcom material. But they convinced Jesus and His motley crew to stay in their home, and a beautiful friendship developed.

Our first principle comes to us from Martha. What can we learn about fostering friendships from Luke 10:38? List everything you see.

Those girls didn't fully understand Jesus' identity. They just knew He was an exceptional guy worth knowing. In the category of Picking Great Friend Candidates, they got an A+. And we need to give them props on that because Jesus was losing popularity faster than the Atkins Diet. They weren't seeking friends to advance their position or wealth. They were after a spiritual connection, and nothing less than Jesus would do.

Oh, Girls, I can't say with a clear conscience that the same is true for me. I've pursued people for what they could give me and turned a blind eye to their spiritual condition. "What do I care if she rejects God if she can make me popular? Who cares about her faith? She's so much fun, and I like fun. She can make me seem important. She can pull strings for me that I need to have pulled. I want to rub elbows with her. I need someone who won't call me out spiritually. Plus, church people get on my nerves."

Is anybody feeling me?

*What are your closest friends like? In general, how would you describe them spiritually?

What draws you to them?

I hope you hear the difference between this and loving the lost. No doubt we should be neck deep in people who need Jesus, but our role is to point Him out, show them His kindness. Jesus spent time with sinners constantly, but they were around Him only eight minutes before asking Him to fix them up. He never angled for position or wasted time posturing. In every relationship He engaged in, Jesus had an eye on eternity.

We look at this passage and see an encounter with divinity. This touch from the Son of God is the stuff of Bible stories. Yet on a real level, this is the way any new friendship begins: dinner, a warm home, good conversation. "Come on over, Jesus. I'll make You some soup. I want to know You."

Hospitality is the breeding ground for deep friendships. Not entertaining—that puts the emphasis on appearances and requires performing. We put on a show to entertain, try to channel Martha Stewart. Entertaining aims for applause from the guests, not intimacy. Hospitality says, "Come over for coffee. Let's sit on the back porch. Tell me who you are."

My first friend in Austin, Ann Terese, rescued me from apartment despair with my two-year-old son and five-month-old daughter. Recognizing insanity when it trembled, "Yes, we're fine. Austin is great," she invited me over. The conditions were simple: Throw on a hat and flip-flops; your kids can come in jammies; I'll make grilled cheese sandwiches. I spent countless hours at her house. This is how the dearest friends are made: When she didn't put on airs, I didn't have to either.

Do you ever initiate new friendships? Why or why not?

*Is hospitality natural or hard for you? Why do you say that?

Hospitality doesn't come naturally for me. I worry about irrelevant details; my drift is to impress. Is the house immaculate? Is the coffee perfect? Are my kids acting like derelicts? Can she see that dust bunny? Yet when I've pushed those aside and welcomed someone in to know her, not impress her, I've never been sorry. When I resist my prideful motives and selfish agenda, God uses the space to foster a real connection. Solomon warned in Proverbs 12:9,

> Better to be ordinary and work for a living
> than act important and starve in the process. (MSG)

With other women, do you act ordinary, or do you just act?

Has your façade left you starving for real friends? Don't lie to yourself.

Hospitality was standard in Jesus' culture. Traveling rabbis and their students stayed in homes everywhere they journeyed. In fact, the Pirke Avat 1:4, a collection of wisdom from Jesus' time, said, "Let your house be a meeting place for the rabbis, and cover yourself in the dust of their feet, and drink in their words thirstily."[1]

Hmmmm.

Luke goes on to tell us, "She had a sister called Mary, who sat at the Lord's feet listening to what he said" (Luke 10:39). Jesus wasn't making idle chitchat. He went straight to deep.

We know this because six months later, the only person on earth who understood His death was Mary. I imagine Jesus told her about His divinity and the sin that separates and how He wanted to bridge the gap. And as Mary sat there, getting dust from Jesus' feet on her clothes where she knelt, she understood Him.

Read Luke 10:40-42. What kind of Savior is Jesus? What can you learn about His desire here?

Martha chose entertaining; Mary chose hospitality. Martha chose to work for Jesus; Mary chose to know Him. It's clear which had more value. I love this principle of friendship because life is too short to live on the surface. Flitting around, talking about nothing important drains me to the core. Conventional wisdom says honest conversations exhaust us, but I couldn't disagree more.

Karla Worley wrote,

> "Know me" is the cry of a woman's heart. . . . At some point in a true relationship, we choose to be this kind of journey-friend: We choose to know each other this well. A friendship, like any other relationship, has its stages. We meet. We are attracted to each other. We fall in love. Telling my story is a part of the falling in love stage. . . . Some people can't get beyond this telling-my-story stage. But there is a point at which it's time to write "the rest of the story"—the point at which you choose to go on, to travel together.[2]

 Which stage do you fall in with most of your friends? If you get stuck, why is that?

*What would you say to a woman who sees only incredibly busy women around her who couldn't possibly have time to be her friend?

Intimacy can be scary. Real friends can't be fooled by the polished you, all shined up and presentable. They see you when you're rusted or a little broken. They know some parts of you are held together with duct tape. They might discover you're one big bag of mess.

But so are they.

Women the world over need another woman they can be real around. No one can be honest around a girl who never shows her cards. Superficial friends are a dime a dozen, but a real friend is a treasure. Friendship like this never happens on the surface. It's a place of depth, like Mary and Jesus had. Martha tried to impress Him with the polished her, but He preferred a friend who listened, who sat with Him without posturing. He didn't need fancy food or designer dishes. He wanted time. He wanted authenticity. He wanted a real friend.

Love that Jesus.

Lonely?

1. Choose a good-friend candidate with a heart for Jesus.
2. Try to set aside one hour this month. Will you try?
3. Invite her over. Have some coffee. No need to impress.
4. Talk. Listen. Share your stories.
5. Be willing to progress to the deep. Jesus says it's better there.

Do you need to release some hang-ups here? Pray for a name, a new friendship to initiate. Ask God to show you any unhealthy friendships or motives.

The Deep End

I love girlfriends. I love them on my back porch with our feet kicked up. I love them while we devour chips and salsa. I love them when we're taking a road trip. I love them when they call to analyze an episode of *American Idol*. These moments hold immense value. Though they appear casual, they hold the supernatural because they prepare a friendship for crisis.

My girlfriends and I have laughed together more than anything. But we've also rallied around our friend suffering from panic attacks. We've held her hand to victory. These same girls smothered my family when my daughter began having seizures. We cried and prayed through our friend's infertility. We closed in like vultures when one friend shared, "My marriage is in trouble."

I think Jesus preferred the deep end of friendship for this reason. In fact, Paul told us to "carry each other's burdens, and in this way you will fulfill the law of Christ" (Galatians 6:2). Now, that's a law worth following, Girls.

Read John 11:1-3. (We'll deal with verse 2 later this week.) In crisis, do you prefer people who love you or a compassionate acquaintance or pastor? Why?

The sisters didn't have to ask Jesus to come. They were so certain of His love for their brother that they only sent word of his sickness. See, between real friends, there is a safety net of the assumed. When we say, "I'm hurting," we know our friends will come. They'd never leave us alone in crisis, whether we ask for their presence or not. This is one reason to allow yourself to be loved deeply. When calamity comes—and it will—you'll stand together.

Have your true friends gathered around you in a crisis? When?

Read John 11:4-6. The NASB says, "Now Jesus loved Martha and her sister and Lazarus. So when He heard that he was sick, He then stayed two days longer in the place where He was" (verses 5-6). How could Jesus' delay be evidence of His love for these friends?

Women rarely make this decision. Friend in trouble? We're there with a casserole in thirty-two minutes. We swoop in quick. Women are fixers of pain; if we can't eliminate it, we'll take it on ourselves. Many times this is precisely what our friend needs. But sometimes we stunt our friend's growth process by removing something uncomfortable that God put there on purpose.

A good litmus test is our fatigue level. When we take on God's work in a friend's life, it's an unhealthy burden. We are not big enough to fill God's shoes, so when we try, we end up discouraged and exhausted. There is certain friend-work He delegates to us, but there are deep places of brokenness He alone is capable of fixing. I've discovered this by working myself to fatigue with no results in the life of my friend. I've learned that sometimes all I can say is, "I love you. I'm praying, and I'm here."

Karla Worley explained this stance:

> Sometimes "being there" means not being there. A time to embrace, says Ecclesiastes 3, and a time to refrain from embracing. There is a time when being there means giving your friend space, giving her wings. . . . "Being there" does not make me her Savior. In fact, when I try to save her, I keep her from knowing the One who is her Savior. . . . Do you trust God enough to let your friend go through the trial? Do you trust God enough to wait in the darkness of the cross, the tomb—when hope has died? Do you trust that He is bringing about new life?[3]

It's no mystery that God uses extreme circumstances for His glory. Find me one major Bible character who didn't go through the fire. Yes, those flames burn, but they also purify. They burn off self-reliance, pride, doubt. We are left cleaner than before, more moldable than ever. So when we snatch our girlfriends out of the flames too quickly, we can short-circuit their spiritual maturity and rob God of the glory He should've had.

*Do you ever get overwhelmed thinking you should solve all your friends' problems? Or do you expect them to fix all your issues?

Has this pressure affected the way you do friendship? How?

Read John 11:7-17. Had Jesus come and healed Lazarus, it would have been a common miracle. Do you see a correlation between Jesus' affection for him and the miracle He was setting up? What can we learn from this?

Jesus was a day's walk away. Some other dear friend volunteered to take the message to Him. So between the journey there, two days of delay, and Jesus' walk to Bethany, Lazarus had been dead four days. Jewish custom provided for three days of very heavy mourning, then four of heavy mourning, followed by lighter mourning for the remainder of thirty days.[4] By the time Jesus got there, He'd missed Lazarus' decline, his death, his burial, and the worst of his sisters' pain.

Read John 11:18-27. From this exchange, what do you think Jesus was trying to accomplish in Martha?

I love this about Jesus. Nothing is wasted on His watch, nor is it by chance. By golly, He just won't leave us in our immaturity. Sometimes we wish He would, because the path to progress is often prickly. But He prefers our spiritual growth over our comfort. Martha wanted Jesus four days ago, but He was looking further down the road. Four days ago, she would've declared, "You are the Healer." But today she would say, "You are the Resurrection."

Maturity.

There is nothing better we can do for our friends than challenge their faith. Human nature would choose stagnation, the road more traveled for sure. It's why we favor friends who justify our choices rather than confront them.

Jesus asked Martha, "Do you believe this?" We need to ask our girlfriends the same question and throw in some others: "What are you learning in the Word? What are you struggling with? How can I pray for you? What do you think God is trying to teach you?" This is what real friends in Christ do. Anything less removes our distinction, and we become like every other relationship apart from Jesus.

*Do you open up your spiritual life to your friends? Do you hold anything back? Why?

If this seems optional to you (or impossible), dig deep and identify the emotion that keeps you spiritually pretending.

Fear? Pride? Self-sufficiency? Believer, none of those come from God. Your Enemy is at the root of your isolation. If he can keep the family of God fragmented in dishonesty and pretense, then we're only as strong as the one link we represent. Super for Satan, devastating for Jesus. Jesus would have us in honest community because it creates an army of holiness, a force to be reckoned with. "You coming after me, Satan? You'll have a whole gaggle of girls to deal with. Good luck to you."

In our story, Jesus extracted a confession of faith from Martha. He needed this sit-down with her. She didn't give Him that opportunity earlier, as she was too busy in the kitchen. Jesus hadn't shared His secrets with her as He did with Mary at His feet. Crisis forced her hand, though. She was ready to listen. And she did.

With that, He sent for Mary.

Read John 11:28-34. The girls said the same thing to Jesus, but notice the two different ways He responded. What do you make of this?

Oh, Girls, there is nothing sweeter than knowing Jesus. Spending time listening at His feet frees Him up to work wonders in our lives. Some of us are missing miracles because we're forcing Jesus to spend all His time convincing us of His power. Mary didn't need a lesson on His divinity in the moment of crisis. She'd already learned it in the comfort of her living room. When our relationship with Jesus is marked

by disobedience and discipline, we can't enter the realm of the marvelous as quickly.

This doesn't mean we have to become perfect; it means we have to become perfectly still. Spend time at Jesus' feet and listen as He pours life into your spirit. Discover grace. Experience His shocking love for you. Let Him teach you who He is. Walk with Him through His Word. When Jesus knows you know Him, the two of you get to write the rest of your story. It's the ultimate design of friendship, and Jesus is the reigning champ.

> "No longer do I call you slaves, for the slave does not know what his master is doing; but I have called you friends, for all things that I have heard from My Father I have made known to you." (John 15:15, NASB)

 How is the spiritual health of your friendships? Pray over your friends and ask for discernment for each one.

Jesus' Little Helpers

My Girlfriend Leslie and her dear husband, Robert, were neck deep in adopting a baby girl from China last year. If you've been privy to this process, you know how laborious it is. I wanted to pull my hair out walking the journey with Leslie, as patience has never been my long suit.

A month from the end, the adoption agency called to say they'd send the first picture of their daughter via e-mail that day. Well, as girlfriends go, we're a tight bunch. Once that news traveled the circuit, we dropped what we were doing and descended on her house to wait for the picture. It was like being in the waiting room while our friend was having a baby, only without the bonus of drugs.

We checked e-mail every five minutes, and it just wouldn't come. Finally, *finally* the file showed up in her inbox. We held our breath, and up popped the most beautiful baby girl bundled up like the Michelin Man. I kid you not, all the girlfriends screamed like we'd just won the lottery. There were tears aplenty, and we obsessed over every detail for an hour. Baby Lily was coming, and we all laid claim to her. Because we all lay claim to Leslie.

God created women for friendship. I'm convinced. We can transfer feelings to a friend or take a portion of her emotions on. Empathy is a natural current that flows freely among girls. Our Jesus was so good at balancing strong masculinity with tenderness. He jumped into the deep end of compassion all the time. But perhaps no example is as precious as the resurrection of Lazarus.

Read John 11:33-37. Review Jesus' words that the messenger brought the sisters in verses 3-4. What do you think Mary and Martha were thinking now that Jesus was there?

Dear Girls, if you've never really loved Jesus, I pray that today your heart is rendered. Matthew Henry wrote, "Tears of devout affection have a voice, a loud prevailing voice, in the ears of Christ; no rhetoric like this. . . . Christ gave this proof of his humanity, in both senses of the word; that, as a man, he could weep, and, as a merciful man, he *would weep*, before he gave this proof of his divinity."[5]

We never read of Jesus laughing, but we find Him groaning, crying, grieving for His beloved friends. He was completely undone with compassion. I can see Him reaching out, embracing Mary and Martha in sorrow, looking at the other tear-stained faces, and dropping to His knees, His tears making mud drops in the dirt. His emotions were so strong that the other Jews said with wide eyes, "See how he loved him!" (verse 36).

What a friend we have in Jesus, all our sins and griefs to bear.

Believer, as His ambassadors, we must come up under our friends and feel their feelings with them. To shed tears with our girlfriends is to take part in Jesus' ministry of new life. There is something supernatural there. Our friends can

literally release some of their pain when we carry it for them. In doing so, we tell them:

"You're not alone." *Release*.
"Your feelings are justified." *Release*.
"I hear you." *Release*.
"I'll help see you through." *Release*.

 When was the last time you felt an emotion on behalf of your friend? What effect did it have on her? (Don't know? Ask her.)

Or are you guarded in this area? If so, can you say why?

Same goes for our joys. Real friends are as glad to share your victories as your sorrows. They probably journeyed with you to get there anyway. Henry David Thoreau wrote of these friends: "They cherish each other's hopes. They are kind to each other's dreams."[6] My girlfriends are so kind to my dreams. Thank you, Dear Ones.

This should be natural, but we have an enemy called Pride. Pride sometimes rears its yucky head when our friend experiences success. *What if she's doing better than me now? What if I get left behind? What if she becomes wealthier, more confident? Who is going to be a mess with me?* Pride gets stuck looking inward and can't see our friend's success for the joy it is. It's easier to travel our friends' valleys than their mountaintops; then we know we're doing better than someone else.

Have you experienced negative emotions at a friend's success? Can you pinpoint why you felt that way?

Read John 11:38-44. This is the fourth and fifth time Jesus referenced their belief (verses 40 and 42). What did Jesus want them to believe so much?

Let's turn toward the other friends. Verse 19 told us that "many Jews had come to Martha and Mary to comfort them." As Jesus surveyed the scene, their tears moved Him to a disturbed spirit. See, Jesus was the girls' friend, but His days were numbered. So for the actual miracle, He enlisted the help of their other friends, a living sermon on the "cords of human kindness" (Hosea 11:4).

"Take away the stone." That's the first thing He ordered in verse 39. Jesus made a habit of using other people in His miracles. "Remove the stone. Fill the jars with water. Pass out the baskets of fish and bread. Bring your friend to Me." Jesus will do the miracle, but we are His fellow workers (1 Corinthians 3:9).

This is our job as a friend in Christ. We serve our friend; we do some of the heavy lifting. We listen to Jesus' instruction and pave the way for Him to work His miracles. What stone can you remove in your friend's life? How can you help physically so He can help spiritually? Maybe you cook for her family, clean her bathrooms, watch her kids, take something off her plate. Sometimes this grunt work seems insignificant, but this was indeed Jesus' pattern: "Roll away the stone; I'll resurrect what's dead."

*What is your experience with servant friends? What is a tangible way you've served a friend? Or how have you been served?

Do you have a friend who needs you like this right now? What can you do?

Again, time. I know. Just remember this: The time you give your job and family is *not* on par with the time you give your friends. It is impractical to attempt equal balance in your roles; some are simply more demanding. For our purposes, balance

means each role has a place in your life; no one role is crowded out entirely by another.

Friendship is definitely a smaller piece of the pie, so just begin where you are. One hour a month? Two? A bimonthly breakfast? Weekly lunch date? Playgroup? Coffee and dessert after the kids go to bed?

I schedule friend time like I do everything else. My neighbors and I have a Tuesday morning playgroup. My girlfriends and I meet for Thursday lunch with our kids. For now, that's where it makes sense in my schedule, but you may be doing great to give one hour a month to a friend. Again, you know your schedule and your goals. Make them work for you.

"What concerns you in this area?

What time can you set aside for friendship? What will you try?

Certainly there are seasons when friends take a major backseat, but Believer, we need each other. Solomon was so right:

> Two are better than one,
>   because they have a good return for their work:
> If one falls down,
>   his friend can help him up.
> But pity the man who falls
>   and has no one to help him up! (Ecclesiastes 4:9-10)

Jesus talked about love and community as much as any subject. He was a living demonstration of fellowship.

Jesus called, "Lazarus, come out!" (John 11:43). Jesus still breathes life back into death, even when it appears so dead that it's already decaying. No marriage is too far gone, regardless of your opinion. No soul is too ruined for redemption. There isn't

one of our children so far removed from Christ that he can't be found. There's not a relationship beyond repair.

Jesus asks us, "Do you believe this?"

Lazarus walked out of the grave, and again Jesus used his friends: "Take off the grave clothes and let him go" (verse 44). As believers, we must walk our friend out of her tomb. We'll gently help remove what has bound her so tightly. We'll stand beside Jesus and help however He tells us to. If we don't try, we don't really love her. We can't create new life, but we can roll away stones.

And if the grave has your name on it, please listen as Jesus calls you back to the living. Receive the hands that help Him; Jesus works through cords of human kindness. Let your girl-friends remove your bindings. I know it's too bright at first, and moving around is hard after tomb-dwelling, but Jesus stands at the entrance where your friends have rolled away the stone.

Believer, what is the deadest circumstance in your life? Maybe in the life of your friend? Ask Jesus to show you how you can help. If you need the help, pray for Jesus to work His miracle through the love of your friends. Receive it, Dear One.

The Great Exchange

It used to drive me crazy to finish a study or book and not remember half of what I learned. I've come to terms with that in two ways:

1. Not every word is my aha truth. I approach each study with some parts of my life healthy and other parts borderline inpatient. So my takeaways are going to be in the areas I need them. So are yours. If you walk away armed for progress in your problem areas, it was time well spent.
2. Reviewing and compiling learned information makes me ten times more likely to retain it. Going back, remembering, summarizing—this process helps me turn good information into something usable.

Today we're going to roll up our sleeves and do just that. We'll go back through your journaling and answers and find out what your aha moments were. Yes, I know this takes a little work, but I can't tell you how valuable this process is. With the information you compile, you'll make a workable schedule

tomorrow to implement the changes you red-flagged.

Begin with prayer and ask for discernment. Ask the Spirit to make your relationships and commitments clear today. Go through the list that follows and fill in your personal responses. Go back through your book and journal to remember. If an area is healthy or it doesn't apply to you, leave it blank. Don't force an issue if there isn't one.

In your journal or on a separate sheet of paper, write your responses to each question pertaining to your role as a *believer*. Be brief. Get right to the point.

- What attitude needs to go?
- What baggage is Satan holding me back with?
- What unrealistic expectations do I need to release?
- Who am I trying to please or impress?
- What is stealing my time from this role/relationship?
- Where am I overcommitted?
- Where do I need to delegate or set limits in this role/relationship?
- What discussion or confrontation do I need to initiate?
- What specific time will I commit to foster this relationship?
- What is the number one thing God wants for me in this role?

Now go through the same process for each of the following roles (skip any that don't apply to you):

- Wife
- Mom
- Professional
- Daughter
- Friend

Oh, Girls, you may have nothing but blanks, but God has shown me where I was way out of whack. Over the course of this project, I withdrew from three commitments, pulled my kids out of a weekly obligation, said no half a dozen times, reorganized my daily schedule, enlisted the domestic help of the four people who live with me, drew some boundaries with a friend, and created some new professional limits.

You want to know something? I feel better.

I really do. Granted, I had to accept that a life well lived is busy. That may sound ridiculous, but I kept thinking the right formula or scheduling methods would finally make me not busy. I'd put my feet up, take a deep breath, and live my new, serene life. What I've discovered is that a growing relationship with the Lord, a passionate marriage, healthy motherhood, a thriving career, and engaged friendships take a lot of work. There is no shortcut. But I'm going to work to either exhaustion or to productivity.

I also learned that most of my fatigue comes from relationships that are injured or unhealthy. When I'm at odds with God, the wheels come off. Same goes for my husband; as long as we're enjoying each other, my workload seems less overwhelming. And so it goes. For me, 75 percent of the battle is emotional. The other 25 percent has to do with organization and time management.

On the first day of this study, we read words God spoke to restore His people after seventy years of captivity. As they shook off the heartache of bondage, God gently promised, "Those who hope in the LORD will renew their strength" (Isaiah 40:31). He is faithful in His promises, Believer. Remember that *renew* literally means "to exchange." He can replace our tired, old exhaustion for strength and joy. He can do that, but you have to hand it over. God can't exchange what you won't release to Him.

Look over your list from today. Pray over each role one by one. Open your hands to God and ask for an exchange: "God, I'd like to exchange our relationship of fear and obligation for one of grace. Lord, I'd like to trade in my fragmented marriage for the one you had in mind. Jesus, I'm trading in my Mom Guilt for confidence so my kids can enjoy me again." Hand it over, Friend. Hand it all over.

> Do you not know?
>> Have you not heard?
> The LORD is the everlasting God,
>> the Creator of the ends of the earth.
> He will not grow tired or weary,
>> and his understanding no one can fathom.
> He gives strength to the weary
>> and increases the power of the weak.
>> (Isaiah 40:28-29)

DAY FIVE

Redemption

My Girlfriends in Christ, let's bring it all down to something tangible, a foundation for a more balanced life. Great intentions plus $3.78 will buy you a White Chocolate Mocha Latte at Starbucks. Let's become women who move conviction out of the dormant state of ideas into the active phase of change.

I want to share some of God's good truth with you. Through Paul, God gave some hardcore advice for living well:

> Look carefully then how you walk! Live purposefully and worthily and accurately, not as the unwise and witless, but as wise (sensible, intelligent people), Making the very most of the time [buying up each opportunity], because the days are evil. Therefore do not be vague and thoughtless and foolish, but understanding and firmly grasping what the will of the Lord is. (Ephesians 5:15-17, AMP)

This version urges us to make the very most of the time. Other translations put it like this:

- "Make the most of every chance you get." (MSG)
- "Walk circumspectly . . . redeeming the time." (KJV)
- "Make the best use of your time." (NLV)
- "Make every minute count." (CEV)

None of us plans on being vague and thoughtless and foolish with our time. It just happens. Forgive the cliché, but if you don't schedule your time, someone will schedule it for you. That's how most of us got where we are. One commitment turned to four, a careless yes added something else, distraction allowed us to slam our kids with too many activities, and bam! Our family is the center attraction at the Freak Show Circus.

So in the name of purpose, worth, and wisdom, let's reclaim our time. I'm giving you permission to say "no," "we're pulling out," "I need a replacement," "I can't come," "I'm using this time for my marriage," "I'm spending the next thirty minutes reading in my chair," "don't ask me to help with ____," "my kids aren't doing this." Oswald Chambers wrote, "The good is always the enemy of the best."[7] Let's choose the best and say no to every other thing that steals us away from it.

Look back over your aha moments from yesterday. This is your best. These are the relationships and roles that matter most. In the following calendar, fill in your schedule *the way it looks now.* Include daily obligations such as Bible study or cleaning (use a pencil). Also include weekly, monthly, or bimonthly commitments. Write in everything and everyone you give your time to. If you have some intangibles (frequent phone calls, e-mailing, pop-in visits), write them on the calendar where they usually occur—daily, weekly, or monthly. Be thorough.

Now review the time stealers you identified yesterday, whether they belong to you or your family members (an extraneous commitment, a kids' activity, a toxic relationship, any waste of time). If you're willing to weed out, go through

your calendar and mark those out. Girls, be ruthless. Refuse to settle for anything less than best. If you are thinking of rearranging any of your time, write that in. Literally redeem your time.

Now look again at the people and commitments that deserve your time: quality time with your kids every day, time with the Lord, date nights with your hubby, girlfriend time, work time, bubble bath time (it was on my list, so I gave it to you). Look discerningly at your daily, weekly, and monthly schedules and fill in those commitments.

When are you meeting with God in His Word? When are you a captive audience for your kids? What night are you going out with your husband? Monthly Girls' Night Out? Weekly coffee? Family night twice a month? How much sex each week? (You know it's easier when we plan for it.) When does work begin and end? What's your house-cleaning plan—daily, weekly? Did you schedule time with a counselor? When do you serve God out of your overflow? Do you meet with a small group of believers? During which activities will you turn your phone off? When are you going to care for yourself, and how will you do that (exercise, reading time, walking, nightly baths)?

Schedule your time so no one else will. Organize your days so they're working for you, not against you. Make some hard choices for your kids; no one will protect their time but you. Don't teach them to spin out in exhaustion.

But please don't turn this into a yoke of bondage. If you miss something here or there, no big deal. Accept that real life deals out plenty of unexpected time stealers. It is what it is. But as much as it depends on you, you'll be proactive, not reactive.

I hope you caught the last part of Ephesians 5:17. Reclaiming your time leads to "understanding and firmly

grasping what the will of the Lord is" (AMP). Isn't that what we're all looking for? There is no better life than what God has in mind for you—no bigger dream, no better family, no healthier marriage, no deeper friendships. Making every second count leads you to that place. Believer, that is the place of renewed strength. That is a life filled with the best, not distracted by too many goods.

Dear Girlfriend, will you choose His will? Will you eliminate the fillers that keep you from a life of purpose? He stands with you. This isn't work you have to do by yourself, but it's what you must hand over to the One who is able. He has never once wasted an offering.

Thank you for letting me walk alongside you. I hope we meet someday. You'll recognize me: I'll be the one not losing my time anymore. I'm sure you will be, too. I'll look for a spring in your step and a twinkle in your eye.

Comfort, comfort my people,
    says your God.
Speak tenderly to Jerusalem,
    and proclaim to her
that her hard service has been completed.
    (Isaiah 40:1-2)

Notes	Sunday	Monday	Tuesday

Wednesday	Thursday	Friday	Saturday

Leader's Guide

For this study, each woman will need:

1. A copy of *Make Over*
2. A Bible (most references included come from the NIV)
3. A journal or notebook with lined paper

Make Over is a six-week study. Each week requires five days of work. Women will spend approximately thirty minutes on each day of Bible study.

It's always helpful if the leader has some familiarity with the Bible passages. I suggest that leaders stay a week ahead in the study in order to offer advance guidance if necessary. The ideal size for a small group is eight to twelve women.

The small-group discussion should take sixty to ninety minutes, depending on the size and personality of the group. Feel free to supplement that time with worship, activities, or a large-group session.

Each week, set the example by having your Bible and book open and ready. Begin each session with prayer, asking God to inhabit your conversation and increase your faith.

Have your girls open their books to Days 1–4. The questions marked with an asterisk (*) are good discussion questions to pose. There are two to four of them marked in each day of study. Look ahead at the designated questions to prepare adequately for discussion. Most of the questions selected involve personal application of the study, but by all means keep bringing in the Scripture and history that set them up.

If your group obviously wants to pursue a different point, don't squash the Spirit's leading. Create an atmosphere of authenticity by voicing your own thoughts and struggles. Keep conversation moving and work hard to include all four days in discussion. If you aim to spend roughly fifteen minutes on each day's questions, Days 1–4 will take about an hour to cover.

When Days 1–4 have been discussed, refer to Day 5. As this is a personal prayer and journaling activity, wrap up your conversation by asking, "What was the biggest thing you took away from this day? This week? What did the Spirit teach you in prayer and journaling?"

Close each session in prayer. Brainstorm creative prayer techniques with other leaders. Use Scripture, music, silence, prompts, partner praying, guided silent prayer; any format that brings women together in prayer should be a primary goal for your group.

Notes

WEEK ONE: JACKED UP

1. Sheila Wray Gregoire, *To Love, Honor, and Vacuum* (Grand Rapids, MI: Kregel, 2003), 50.
2. Carol E. Lee, "Editorial Observer: The Evolution of Women's Roles, Chronicled in the Life of a Doll," *The New York Times*, March 30, 2004, http://select.nytimes.com/search/restricted/article?res=F70813FE3D5D0C738FDDAA0894DC404482.
3. Donald Miller, *Searching for God Knows What* (Nashville: Nelson, 2004), 108–109.
4. Bill Thrall, Bruce McNicol, and John Lynch, *TrueFaced* (Colorado Springs, CO: NavPress, 2004), 16.
5. "English Bible History: Martin Luther," http://www.greatsite.com/timeline-english-bible-history/martin-luther.html.
6. Miller, 159.
7. Thrall, McNicol, and Lynch, 53.

WEEK TWO: BELIEVER

1. Donald Miller, *Searching for God Knows What* (Nashville: Nelson, 2004), 156.
2. "The KJV Old Testament Hebrew Lexicon," crosswalk.com, http://bible.crosswalk.com/Lexicons/Hebrew/heb.cgi?number=01058.

3. *NIV Study Bible* (Grand Rapids, MI: Zondervan, 2002), 147.

4. *NIV Study Bible*, 374.

5. Bill Thrall, Bruce McNicol, and John Lynch, *TrueFaced* (Colorado Springs, CO: NavPress, 2004), 51–52.

Week Three: Wife

1. *The American Heritage Dictionary of the English Language*, 4th ed., s.v. "affection," http://dictionary.reference.com/browse/affection.

2. Sheila Wray Gregoire, *To Love, Honor, and Vacuum* (Grand Rapids, MI: Kregel, 2003), 94.

3. "The Good Wife's Guide," *Housekeeping Monthly*, May 13, 1955, http://www.snopes.com/language/document/goodwife.asp.

4. Gregoire, 96–97.

5. Dr. Henry Cloud and Dr. John Townsend, *Boundaries* (Grand Rapids, MI: Zondervan, 1992), 156.

6. First two examples from Cloud and Townsend, *Boundaries*, 157.

7. Dr. Henry Cloud and Dr. John Townsend, *Boundaries in Marriage* (Grand Rapids, MI: Zondervan, 1999), 149.

8. Ontario Consultants on Religious Tolerance, "U.S. Divorce Rates for Various Faith Groups, Age Groups, and Geographic Areas," http://www.religioustolerance.org/chr_dira.htm, citing Barna Research Group, "Christians Are More Likely to Experience Divorce Than Are Non-Christians," December 21, 1999, http://www.barna.org/cgi-bin/.

9. Gregoire, 92.

10. Gregoire, 183.

11. Shaunti Feldhahn, *For Women Only* (Sisters, OR: Multnomah, 2004), 156.

12. Feldhahn, 162–163.

13. Feldhahn, 93–94.

14. Feldhahn, 100.

WEEK FOUR: MOM

1. *NIV Study Bible* (Grand Rapids, MI: Zondervan, 2002), 362.

2. Ray C. Stedman, "Ruth: The Romance of Redemption," *Peninsula Bible Church Library*, November 15, 1964, http://www.pbc.org/dp/stedman/adventure/0208.html.

3. Sheila Wray Gregoire, *To Love, Honor, and Vacuum* (Grand Rapids, MI: Kregel, 2003), 120–121.

4. Rusty Russell, "The Moabite Stone," *Bible History Online*, http://www.bible-history.com/resource/ff_mesha.htm.

5. *Easton's Bible Dictionary*, s.v. "Redemption," http://eastonsbibledictionary.com/r/redemption.htm.

6. Josh Weidmann, *Dad, If You Only Knew* (Sisters, OR: Multnomah, 2005), 95, 97–98.

WEEK FIVE: PROFESSIONAL AND DAUGHTER

1. Dr. Henry Cloud and Dr. John Townsend, *Boundaries* (Grand Rapids, MI: Zondervan, 1992), 196.

2. Cloud and Townsend, *Boundaries*, 199.

3. *The Quotations Page*, http://www.quotationspage.com/quote/29007.html.

4. Cloud and Townsend, *Boundaries*, 134–135.

5. "Quick Search Results," *BibleGateway.com*, http://www.biblegateway.com/quicksearch/?quicksearch=sabbath&qs_version=31.

WEEK SIX: FRIEND

1. Lois A. Tverberg, "Raise Up Many Disciples!" *En-Gedi Resource Center, Inc.*, 2002, http://www.en-gedi.org/articles/director/articles_director_0602.html.

2. Karla Worley, *Traveling Together* (Birmingham, AL: New Hope Publishers, 2003), 55, 64.

3. Worley, 91, 103, 105.

4. *NIV Study Bible* (Grand Rapids, MI: Zondervan, 2002), 1615.

5. Matthew Henry, "Commentary on John 11," *Matthew Henry Complete Commentary on the Whole Bible*, http://bible. crosswalk.com/Commentaries/MatthewHenryComplete/mhc -com.cgi?book=joh&chapter=011.

6. "Famous Quotations by Henry David Thoreau," *Quotationz .com*, http://www.quotationz.com/author.asp?authorID=7235.

7. Oswald Chambers, "The Good or the Best?" in *My Utmost for His Highest*, May 25, 2006, http://www.rbc.org/utmost/index .php?day=25&month=05.

About the Author

Jen Hatmaker has served alongside her husband, Brandon, in full-time ministry for twelve years. Six of those years have been at their current post, Lake Hills Church in Austin, where amazingly no one has asked them to leave. While serving women through teaching and writing, Jen has taken it upon herself to discover whether it's possible to love Jesus wholeheartedly and still have a teeny addiction to reality TV. She and Jesus are still working that one out.

Jen is the mother of three "lively" children, which is a euphemism for loud. Some people say they come by that honestly (from their dad's side, obviously). Gavin (eight), Sydney (six), and Caleb (four) are clearly unimpressed with Jen's speaking and writing; when Sydney peered into Jen's first box of books ever released, she glanced up and asked indifferently, "What's for dinner?"

Jen's girlfriends continue to be collaborators on her various ministry pursuits, such as making sure that right before an event she doesn't get a drastic haircut she's incapable of styling, and covering for her when she spends too much money on a pair of boots ("She needs to look impeccable in front

of a crowd, Brandon."). They are very spiritually mature in these areas, and should you need to borrow them, their phone numbers are listed on Jen's website.

By a sheer act of God, Jen has written four other books, including *A Modern Girl's Guide to Bible Study: A Refreshingly Unique Look at God's Word, Road Trip: Five Adventures You're Meant to Live, Tune In: Hearing God's Voice Through the Static,* and *Girl Talk: Getting Past the Chitchat,* all with NavPress.

Jen would love to speak at your event! To find out more information about her ministry or to contact her, visit her online at www. jenhatmaker.com.

The Navigators is an international Christian organization. Our mission is to advance the gospel of Jesus and His kingdom into the nations through spiritual generations of laborers living and discipling among the lost. We see a vital movement of the gospel, fueled by prevailing prayer, flowing freely through relational networks and out into the nations where workers for the kingdom are next door to everywhere.

NavPress is the publishing ministry of The Navigators. The mission of NavPress is to reach, disciple, and equip people to know Christ and make Him known by publishing life-related materials that are biblically rooted and culturally relevant. Our vision is to stimulate spiritual transformation through every product we publish.

Make Over

Revitalizing the *Many*
Roles You Fill

A Modern Girl's Bible Study
Refreshingly Unique

JEN HATMAKER

NAVPRESS®

BRINGING TRUTH TO LIFE